ALL
BUYE
ARE
LIARS

ALL BUYERS ARE LIARS

EXPOSING THE CLOSELY
GUARDED SECRETS OF ELITE
CAR SALES PROFESSIONALS

SCOTT OWEN

bookshaker

First Published in Great Britain 2009
by www.leanmarketingpress.com

For Dad, who spent years trying to convince me to read, to no avail. The first book I read was his last and I've never looked back. This one is for you, as I will always miss you dearly.

I hope it makes you laugh.

Acknowledgements

My career in the motor trade was built on an almost telepathic understanding with my first sales manager, Shaun Baxter, who taught me the "road to the sale".

I would like to thank Natalie and my children, Ross and Max, for believing in me and forsaking the nicer things in life, on my journey through unemployment.

Andy Sorensen for his consistent support and for shouting about the book, from the rooftops.

Mercedes-Benz for making exceptional cars and allowing me to benefit from their success.

Ashley Lidgard and Pete Tingle for their car buying loyalty.

Nick Graham for his business sense and jaw-dropping dance moves.

Shaun Price and David Coulbeck for their inspirational training.

My brother, for all the carveries.

And finally, my mother, for all her years of worrying.

Debbie Jenkins and Joe Gregory, at Bookshaker, for their publishing guidance and support and for bringing my words to life.

Susan St Maur for her editing prowess, which retained the spirit of the book while discarding the confusion.

Contents

Praise

"All Buyers Are Liars works so well because it sticks two fingers up at the politically correct brigade to lay bare what really happens in the car sales business - whether we like it or not. This book isn't really about the integrity of sales professionals or whether car buyers are, in fact, liars. It's about what separates the truly successful sales people from the rest - including the good stuff, that makes customers love them, and the subtle tricks, that ensure they get the sale, too. Although the author draws on his extensive experience in car sales many of these insider secrets will be just as valuable in any sales scenario. So whether you're a buyer who wants to be one step ahead the next time you're thinking of buying a new car or whether you're a sales professional looking for an edge, this book is definitely worth your time."

Rintu Basu, NLP Trainer and Bestselling author of The Persuasion Skills Black Book, www.thenlpcompany.com

"This book isn't just about selling cars, it's also about ethics, customer care, career management and a whole lot more. Whatever side of the negotiation you find yourself on - whether as a sales professional or a buyer - this book lays out a complete sales roadmap that makes it easier to succeed. All Buyers Are Liars isn't for the faint hearted and belongs in the library of every self respecting sales pro - whatever field you're in."

Simon Hazeldine, Bestselling author of Bare Knuckle Selling & Bare Knuckle Negotiating, www.simonhazeldine.com

"The simple act of buying a car can often seem like a no-holds barred fight. I've met plenty of salesmen in my time who will go to almost any lengths to get the sale. Often though, the customer is just as bad: lying, nit-picking and generally treating the sales professional with contempt from the start. But, there is a better way. This book lays out the good, the bad and the ugly of the car selling business to share the secrets of truly successful car salesmen and women. What's more, as a buyer you'll learn all their tricks so you can use this as your own personal self-defence bible, next time you're on the forecourt. Having bought a Mercedes myself from the author a few years ago, I can vouch that despite the provocative title, he'll show would-be persuasion professionals the right way to win the sale while delighting the customer."

**Ian 'The Machine' Freeman, MMA Fighter,
British Cage Rage Light Heavyweight Champion and Author of
Cage Fighter: The True Story of Ian 'The Machine' Freeman**

Foreword

The stereotypical image of the silver-tongued, suited-and-booted car salesman, out to take the customer for a ride, is so deeply ingrained into the car buyer's mind that the first job a successful car sales professional needs to master isn't even that of gaining trust. The first job is being able to look in the mirror and see a decent person. Your job description doesn't define your value as a human being – your actions do. So, with that first goal in mind, Scott Owen, firmly puts himself on your side, with his fun, if slightly provocative title: *All Buyers Are Liars!*

A top-earning veteran of the auto sales business, Scott drills down into the fundamental skills required to befriend customers, secure deals and keep your manager happy. He provides all the tools and approaches you need to succeed to become an elite car sales professional. Once you have the knowledge contained within this book, you'll be able to develop the attitude and aptitude you need to thrive and survive in the often tough game of car sales.

I have a guiding principle that has served me well during my many years in the automotive sales and leasing industry and now as a trainer and consultant: 'The will to win business is important, but the will to prepare yourself is vital.'

This book succeeds because it combines all the tools you need to develop the right attitude ('the will to win business') with solid tools ('enabling you to be prepared') that will enable you to become a truly exceptional car sales professional.

Shaun Price
Managing Partner Change Creation Ltd
www.changecreation.co.uk

Introduction

For some time I have been intent on publishing my experiences within the motor trade. My intentions grew over the years due to various experiences with customers. These ranged from making me feel that I had mastered the art of persuasion and had been able to help them buy, to the other extreme of not being able to do anything to help the customer, despite their insistence that they wanted to buy.

I have written this book to illustrate the differences between the customer and the seller during a sales process that has stood the test of time. Like the wheel, this process has been around for an eternity without having been re-invented, although it has evolved and been re-interpreted on a massive scale.

I have set out to show you both sides of this process and demonstrate the psychology that is ever present within an industry still perceived to be starved of honesty.

Is it the industry that is dishonest, or indeed is it the customer?

Scott Owen
www.allbuyersareliars.co.uk

Please Note: Throughout this book I have referred to customers and sales people as "him" in addition to the rather vaguer "them." Contrary to popular opinion this is not because all motor traders are male chauvinist pigs, but because it makes the text easier to read. Apologies to the industry's many lady customers who, believe me, can give the sales person a much harder time than any mere man and often are much more knowledgeable, more demanding purchasers.

Sales Process

The sales process was initially developed as a structured system back in the 70's and was called the Pendle system. The entire system was designed to maximise the sale and put customers under pressure to buy. The idea was to gain as much information from the customer as possible, thereby using it against them during negotiation. The main thrust was to gain commitment from them to purchase. Once that had been established a number of further methods ensured that they couldn't fail to agree a deal there and then.

By getting an idea of the customer's requirements, budget and method of payment the sales person would lead the customer in a way by which they would find it difficult to say no. If they then refused to purchase they were reminded of all the things they had said previously to make them feel obliged to purchase anyway, regardless of their true intentions.

Fortunately things are different today; however many of the core elements of this process remain. The industry, having being labelled as dishonest and conniving, has grown to realise that the only way to retain customers' business next time round is to offer the best advice.

The sales process has evolved over the years and is used and taught the world over as the effective way to sell cars as well as other products.

I will illustrate how this process works today, to enable both parties to understand why it's so effective.

Meet & Greet

The meet and greet is exactly as it suggests. This is the initial meeting process between the customer and the sales person. Although the scenario will be different every time, the old adage that "you only have one chance to make a first impression" is key to an effective meet and greet. People make judgements about other people very quickly, often before anything has even been said. This is where the psychology of the sale transaction starts; the moment you look at a prospective customer or the moment they clap eyes on the sales person.

There are a number of methods used by sales people to make that first contact with the prospective customer/victim!

- Straight forward approach, walking up to the customer:
  o "Hi there, how can I help you?"
  o "You OK there? Is there anything I can help with?"
  o "Are you just looking? Or is there anything I can assist you with?"
- Cheeky approach, walking up to the customer:
  o "How many do you want? And what colours?"
  o "If you sit in it you will have to buy it."
- Sneaky method, pretending to be doing something else:
  o "Do you need any help?"
- Stealth approach, hiding behind a car or object (then making them jump):
  o "Hi there!" (then watch them leap)
- Acknowledgement only, non verbal greeting:

- o Quick wave
- o Open smile
- o Nod of the head
- Business card approach:
  - o "I'm (your name). If you need any help come and ask for me."
  - o "Here's my card if you need any help."
- Detached approach:
  - o "Isn't it a lovely / awful day?"
  - o "It's too nice to be working on a day like this."
- Assumptive approach:
  - o "Are you just looking at your new car?"
  - o "Can I take your order?"

Normally the customer's reaction is quite predictable; they will respond in one of two ways:

- "Just looking thanks."
  - o Sales person will respond by:
    - Leaving them alone
    - Asking "are you looking for anything in particular?"
- "Yes I am looking for (specifies)."

Once the introduction has been made it is essential to make the customer feel at ease. This is wholly dependent on how the customer perceives the sales person and what judgement has been made.

At this stage the customer believes he is well within his rights to protect himself (and his wife/girlfriend – hands off!!) against the dreaded sales person. There are plenty of ways the customer can respond, although all are usually predictable.

- "Just looking (yawn)."
- "Just having a browse."
- "Just (this or that)."
- "Don't need any help lad."
- "Yes I am looking for a (specifies)." (Finally)
- Silence, followed by walking off.
- Silence, followed by a look down the nose (as if sniffing some shit on your shoes).
- "I'm OK, just waiting for my wife to finish at Morrison's."

You get the general idea. The first couple of minutes' dialogue will dictate the attitude and behaviour that develops. The use of open questions will get the conversation going. A brief discussion about requirements enables the salesperson to entice the customer to their desk, especially with the offer of freshly brewed Brazilian coffee.

Qualification

The most important part of the process is the qualification of the customer's requirements. There is essential information that should be gained at this early stage, as it will determine the rest of the process. If the sale, or a determined next action, is not concluded at the end of the process, it is the qualification that is to blame.

10 Minutes In Front Of The Fire

Get the customer in and seated comfortably with his freshly made brew. Make them feel at ease and then pummel them with questions. By taking control and asking open questions the customer *should* follow your direction and start to open up.

There are plenty of customers who will have their own agenda and will distract you from your purpose by asking you all the questions. Remember, 10 minutes in front of the fire gives you time to get to know your opponents and learn what kind of people they are. Start reading their body language and mirror their posture and hand gestures. People do this naturally, so I wouldn't be worried that you may look strange. The prospective buyers will also be sussing you out and will judge you on your response to their questions.

This is where the game begins.

The objective of the seller is to find out all about the customer's likes, dislikes, work, values, hobbies, family and anything else they can discover and take note of. As soon as you get information from someone, you find something similar in your own experience that will put you on their level. Building trust and showing empathy will guarantee success in the negotiation stages later on. A customer may not be aware of the buying process and how far down the line of purchase they are, but a professional sales pitch can persuade them to buy and that is the thrill of the chase. How persuasive are you?

The objective of the customer is to gain as much or as little information as they want. The more information they have, the better choice they think they will make, although this isn't always the case. They essentially want to know:

- what car they can get for their money
- how much their part-exchange car is worth
- which finance options are available to them
- how much discount they can get
- what else do they get for their money

All this information gives them a perfect opportunity to compare your prices with those elsewhere and then sneer at you with their results. Also make a mental note: all customers have friends and relatives that know much more than you!

An extremely valuable tool for you here is good questioning, because you use it to tie both sides' needs together. There is no end of good questions you can ask during qualification, but only three – the three ugly sisters - should never be left out. Obviously, how you ask them depends on the individual, and it's wise to intersperse them with other, softer questions.

The Three Ugly Sisters

These are simply the three most used excuses for a customer not to purchase. It is essential to ask these questions at an early stage, on every occasion.

1. Time of Change
    - "When are you thinking of changing your car?"
    - "Are you purchasing this month or sometime in the future?"

2. Budget
   - "How much are you thinking of spending this time?"
   - "What budget have you set yourself?"

3. Decision Makers
   - "Were you thinking of involving anyone else in your decision to buy today?"
   - "Is there anyone else that will help you decide on your purchase?"

They are difficult questions to ask because they are personal and aggressive.

The Time of Change Question...

...can make people recoil, automatically revert to type and back off:

- "Oh, I am not buying today, I am just considering my options."

You can almost hear them shit themselves!

However, you absolutely need to know this right from the start, because if they are not buying for a few weeks or months then what is the point of spending a long time with them? They will be happy to take up your time and use your knowledge and dealership resources. This will assist them in their pursuit of getting the best deal. They will also be happy to get their sticky fingers all over your cars and happily test drive them, using yet more of your time, because this will boost their ego and make them feel good. You don't have to purchase to benefit from retail therapy.

If they are not looking to purchase now, dig a little deeper. Ask them if they would consider an immediate purchase if it is to their financial advantage. Money talks. If they are not receptive to a special deal for now, then get rid of them!

Only kidding; everyone deserves the brand treatment. However do not follow the sales process with customers who are looking to purchase in the future. Offer them a brief overview of the brand, let them have the relevant literature and insist they keep your business card safe; otherwise you will lose them to another salesperson if they do return in the future. Most customers do not see the importance of coming back to you; they have little loyalty, especially at this early stage.

The Budget Question...

...is important because you need to know what product the customer is realistically able to afford, despite their desire for more expensive vehicles. There is no advantage in allowing the customer to decide what they wish to drive or discuss unless you know it is within their budget. This also gives you an opportunity to discuss their preferred payment method, whether that is cash or finance. The trouble here is that you will get the cocky type who wants you to think that money is no object. As we all know, they are lying; money is always an object, especially when it has to be earned. There are also the awkward customers who will be vague and tell you they're not sure how much they want to spend. Make a suggestion and you will soon get a response, usually from their arsehole; it squeaks when you frighten them.

- "Well, did you want to spend £20,000, £40,000 or more?"
- *(Wife's mouth opens in shock) "Oh no, around £10,000 well, maybe up to £15,000."*
- "That's a maximum of £10k then. Good, now we know."

As harsh as it sounds this method works because it surprises people into telling you their real budget and cuts right through the ego buyers. We all like to view things that we can't really afford. However looking is one thing; it is quite another to take up someone's valuable time just to satisfy your fantasy.

So, you have ascertained their budget; now delve a little into how they intend to fund their purchase. Here's a side bet: 80% will say they want to pay cash. This is a usual reaction, similar to the "just looking" response; it tends to be a knee jerk reaction to a personal question. You are asking subliminally if they can afford to buy it or if they will need assistance and some people cannot deal with that intrusion.

Anyway it's bollocks! They are normally borrowing the money from somewhere. Even the cash rich customers do not see the sense in buying a depreciating asset outright, unless they are required to dump some money to stop the tax man getting his filthy hands on it. But don't sweat the small stuff. You're only asking the question at this stage, in the hope that the more honest customer will just tell you his monthly budget requirements instead. Leave it at that. Be happy if you have got a good idea of their budget limitations.

Finding out about the decision makers...

...is the last of the tricky questions. Although it may not seem relevant, believe me and anyone who has ever sold a car, it is. In the long term it isn't, but that is exactly why you need to know now. It will save you going through the whole process of the customer not purchasing because he doesn't have authority from his wife and/or accountant.

It sounds straightforward enough, but there is potential to rub people up the wrong way, which is always fun! See it as a challenge, because essentially you are questioning a customer's ability to make their own decision without consent from their other halves, whichever way round it is. A lot of people are comfortable admitting they need to consult others, which is fine; as long as you know this you can re-appoint them when they are together. It is important to make sure all parties concerned are there to make the eventual decision.

If you have confirmed all three of the ugly sisters then it's a green light. A switched-on salesperson will split the three questions up with another five important but softer questions. This way you are finding other important details out, as well as the critical issues, all at once.

The following questions will give you an example of a sensible flow of information gathering.

- "How much do you know about our brand/company?"
- "What are you driving at the moment?"
- "Are you looking to part-exchange your vehicle?"

- "When are you looking to change your car?"
- "How long do you intend to keep your next car?"
- "And how much are you planning to spend this time?"… "Is that over a period of months?"
- "What do you like about your current car?"
- "Can I ask - who is likely to be involved in the decision?"

By asking open questions in a defined process you can ascertain the essential information without the customer feeling you are only interested in what you can sell them. They will respond because you have established a conversation and most importantly, you are talking about them and asking what they are interested in.

As long as you get the desired response to your critical questions, you can then make a decision about how to move on.

Part-Exchange Appraisal

This is usually a comical part of the process because the customer will inevitably lie or rather exaggerate the facts regarding his car, which may be his pride and joy. It is a time to be sensitive but firm.

Every dealership and used car centre in the land (in their right mind) will have a PX appraisal form. The more information you get the better the valuation and obviously the less you miss, which may cost the business, and you, money.

Treat it as if you are buying the car, because you are representing your company and they are buying the car.

The appraisal form is a great script which allows you to talk about the buyer and their precious car.

I have detailed the information answered by the customer with the correct answer in the following chart. The information also includes the financial cost to the dealership for getting the details wrong, especially the options that the car should have. Note how the information given by the customer always seems to exaggerate their car, rather than doing it an injustice.

QUESTION	CUSTOMER ANSWER	VERIFIED ANSWER	CORRECT OR INCORRECT	VERIFIED ANSWER'S EFFECT ON VALUE
Make	Mercedes-Benz	Mercedes-Benz	Correct	Nil
Model	E280CDi	E280CDi	Correct	Nil
Derivative	Saloon	Saloon	Correct	Nil
Spec. Level	Sport	Avantgarde	Incorrect	-£700
Registration Number	ZA55LVE	ZA55LVE	Correct	Nil
Date of Registration	Think it was Jan 2006	1st Sep 2005	Incorrect	-£500
Mileage	About 25,000	32,564	Incorrect	Negligible due to age

Colour	Metallic Black	Solid Black	Incorrect	-£500 + potential extra damage
Interior Material	Leather (Cream)	Man-made Leather	Incorrect	-£300
Number of Owners	1 (just me)	2 (demo + 1)	Incorrect	-£200
Service History	Full: with franchised dealer	Full: not with franchised dealer	Incorrect	Nil as long as franchise parts used
Last Service	Only just been done	12 months ago	Incorrect	Upto -£1000 depending on service required
MOT	Not required	Expired	Incorrect	-£50 depending on result
Road Fund Licence	Just put a year on it	5 Months	Incorrect	-£100
Damage	No, it's mint!	2 minor scratches + 1 dent	Incorrect	-£200
Options	Everything, fully loaded	Parktronic + Telephone	Incorrect	-£1000 without satellite navigation
Supagard	What's that?	No	Incorrect	Nil but opportunity to mention additional product for discussion later

This illustration does not represent every customer. There are many people who are fastidious about their cars and know everything about them. This example is designed to show the customer's potential for making an error, if you trust everything they tell you.

There are vital checks you will need to do to satisfy your company that certain information is correct and the vehicle is clear of anything untoward.

Once you have gained all the information from the customer take him out to the car and check round the body of the vehicle in front of him. Start with the bonnet, check for scratches, dents and any abrasions. Go round the passenger side of the car, along the back then round the driver's side. As you go round try to estimate the tyre tread levels and look for damage that would require a replacement tyre.

Make sure you inform the owner that you are insured and are required to drive the vehicle and he is welcome to come along. Your benefit here is that while you drive the car you can carry on dialogue with the customer and qualify what he did and did not like about his present vehicle. Press him for reasons why he bought the car in the first place and if he is happy to discuss it, you can ask him what sort of deal he got. It's further qualification and lets you gain valuable knowledge on his buying process, whether he buys on instinct or whether he takes his time and researches thoroughly. Be careful to listen and take in what he is saying. It comes back to being interested in what the customer is looking for, searching for clues as to what they like and dislike.

If this seems repetitive, you're right; it is. Your primary aim throughout the whole process is to keep qualifying the customer persistently, so you learn as much about them and their psychological reasons for buying (known as hot spots) as you can.

I have detailed below the likely truth behind a customer's typical responses; it is quite alarming how different their responses can be when asked fundamental questions about their own car.

The customer's response to the usual facts demonstrates their lack of knowledge of their own vehicle. You can benefit from this due to the fact that you have more knowledge about the car you're selling. Use your own product knowledge to woo them with bits of information about it.

This will build trust because they will realise you have knowledge of your vehicles and your competition. The more trust you build the easier the close becomes. People buy from people, so start plugging away at your customer; make them believe you really are looking after them.

You will need to check the following in every instance:

Service History
- ☐ Check their service book is stamped
- ☐ In its absence, make it a condition of sale to view the service history
- ☐ Note all the services with dates and centre

Damage To The Car

☐ Note all scratches, dents and abrasions
☐ Check interior seat upholstery
☐ Inspect carpets and roof lining
☐ Make sure tools and equipment are present
☐ Ensure tyres are of a required standard
☐ Check windscreen condition for chips and cracks

HPI Approval

Proves car is free from anything untoward, such as:

☐ Finance outstanding
☐ Insurance write-off
☐ Registration change
☐ DVLA investigation
☐ Police register (stolen and un-recovered)
☐ Import

In conclusion, the part-exchange appraisal is designed for you to de-value the customer's car. Make them believe that their car is worth less than they thought, because usually they think it is worth the same value, or more, than you would sell it for. Remember it is their car; they paid for it with their hard-earned money. However also realise that it's never worth as much as they think it is. The aim of a good sales person is to buy it for the minimum possible. This gives you an excellent opportunity to advise them that the value of their car is what another party is willing to offer for it. Towards the end of the process this information can be valuable when negotiating.

I realise that this stage is often misinterpreted. A vast amount of sales people will skim over this part of the process and just note the essential items about the vehicle, failing to analyse the purchase correctly, which often leads to arguments with the management. I can't remember the number of times a car was mis-described, resulting in reduced values being offered from traders looking to buy the part-exchange. If you cut corners it will reduce your chances of getting the message across to your customer.

First Management Review

The first management review is designed to analyse where you are in the process with your customer. You will be expected to report on the feedback you are getting from them. Explain what you have learned so far about their needs and requirements, whether they intend to fund their purchase and offer information on their part-exchange, if applicable. The more details you have the less likely you are to receive a reprimand, because this is usually where negotiations start. It will not be the customer who is talking figures now; it will be your manager!

But stay on track. Remember it is early days and at this stage you are discussing what vehicle will suit the customer and whether you should proceed to present and demonstrate a vehicle to them. A good manager will have his finger on the pulse and should advise a vehicle that will suit the customer as well as the company, such as a car that has been in stock for a number of months. This is an excellent opportunity for a shrewd salesperson to request a fixed commission, usually a lot more than they would pay. Agree which car to demonstrate, or agree that you are not far enough to go any further with them and re-appoint to a convenient date. This is not really a time to delay things, as your customer is going colder while looking around awkwardly in your showroom. Furthermore he inevitably will be nosing around at the things on your desk.

For now let's say you are carrying on down the road to the sale, so get back to your customer.

Presentation

Now that you are getting on famously with your new friends, sorry customers, we can take them to their new car, literally. Firstly though we must prepare; make sure the car is available and on hand. It is best to advise the customer that you are going to bring the car to them, if accessible. If it's jammed behind seventeen other cars you have no choice but to take them to it. You should aim for a five step walk-around.

Get your best face on and start schmoozing.

Bring out the charm and take them to a vehicle.

5 Step Walk-Around

1. Front

Lead the customer to the car from the front, so they can see what they are buying and visualise it on their drive or outside work.

Depending on what you have learned about their likes and dislikes you can describe something that appeals to them, such as the badge, the engine or the crumple zones.

2. Passenger Side

Describe the alloys and tyres or side protection, whichever hits the customers' preference.

Open the passenger door and show them the space, upholstery and ease of access.

Seat them or the spouse in the car. Let them talk about the first things they notice. Listen to the first impressions, they are vital clues.

3. Rear Passenger Seat

Show off the rear space in a saloon or five door model.

Lift the passenger seat forward and show off the rear space. In either case let the customer offer an opinion first; they may criticise something, in which case you can probe further to see if they would indeed require more space than this model is offering.

4. Rear

Show them the rear looks of the car first, reiterating their desires with regards to space.

Open the boot ("trunk" if you're American) or hatch and let them inspect. Don't worry; they will find plenty of things to prod and pull.

5. Driver's Side

Take them round to the driver's side and open the door; give them a glimpse.

Make sure you push the seat and back rest back, to ensure they fix the seat to their own position.

Now offer them the seat, the most important part of the car to them; this is where their dreams begin. Capitalise on this and discuss all the features and benefits that they have said they require.

They will be excited about the prospect of driving the car now and they should not be disappointed. Having planned your presentation and test drive, you will be ready to take them out to build desire further.

Demonstration

Before going anywhere, ask those who intend to drive for their licences. You don't know who these people are and you need to know their information is accurate in case anything happens to the car or yourself. Take a copy of their license and check it against the information they provided. It is at your manager's discretion whether to demonstrate a vehicle if your customer does not have a licence with them. Do not be embarrassed about refusing a demonstration; it is not something a customer is entitled to. There are many people who will disagree with that statement as prospective buyers generally adopt the attitude that they will not buy without driving the vehicle. It is simple; if they intend to buy the vehicle they will return with their licence and carry on the sales process. If they don't return, what were their real intentions in the first place? Driving a nice car about for a bit? Make yourself feel good about yourself? Never driven this brand before? Whatever the reason, this refusal method may sift out some of the time wasters.

Anyway, let's assume that you have copied their licence and the details are correct.

The demonstration should strengthen the desire your customers feel for the car, although some people think that if they say they like it too much this will play into your hands. They are absolutely right, of course; it will. The more they want it, the more easily they will decide and the more they are likely to accept a lower discount. Do you want it sir? Well, do you?

It is good practice for you to drive the vehicle away from the premises. By driving first you can make sure the car is operating as it should (they've been known to conk out or run out of fuel on test drives). It comes back to effective preparation.

As you depart you will travel down a planned route making it easier for someone to find you should anything go pear-shaped. If your managers have not established a set route which incorporates several different road types, then drive round and plan a route yourself. Make sure you tell other people about it though! At least then one of your colleagues can rescue you, should anything mysterious happen. It is valid to mention, in all seriousness, that there is always a risk when you take customers out for a demonstration, such as:

- The car runs out of fuel
- Someone loses control and crashes the car
- The car is stolen on changeover
- One of the passengers pees themselves
- You get hit by a car from behind
- The car catches fire
- You get a puncture
- Your customer knocks you out and drives away
- A football hits your windscreen and shatters it
- One of the passengers vomits

Believe me, all of the above are real examples. Selling cars to the public can be a dangerous life. Be aware!

Once on the road you have a chance to show them the controls and equipment. The easiest way to start is by showing them the important controls like indicators, wipers, lights, mirrors and windows. Try to remember what they said they liked about their current car, which features they mentioned to you when they were boasting. To avoid feature dumping, stick to the items they know about from their own car. Hopefully their new car will have more advanced technology than their part-ex. So tell them how it has advanced; they will be interested because they brought it up before. Then move on to features that they don't have on their old car. A lot of this may have been discussed at the presentation beforehand, but now you have the opportunity to show how it works.

Items such as cruise control can be demonstrated en route. They may not feel comfortable using it themselves but they should know how it can benefit them on certain journeys. This is the time to show the car off so get boasting. Make sure they know the features and the corresponding benefits. You can have some fun and test their knowledge too, depending on how much rapport you feel you have built up. If they say they know about something, open them up and ask them how they use it. You will be surprised at the lack of knowledge people can have about the instruments they see and use every day.

You are still driving the car at this stage so the amount of time for imparting knowledge will depend on the length of your route. A twenty minute journey is considered to be a sensible amount of time to test drive. This is deemed to be acceptable for both parties. The infusion of different types of roads will offer a balanced experience for the customer and leave them feeling able to decide whether they can see themselves owning the car or not. It is up to you to give the best impression of the car before you swap seats.

Pull up safely at your changeover point and turn the ignition off. With some vehicles it is important to show the customer how to operate the handbrake. Certain cars have an alternative system to the usual centrally placed draw-up handle. Most Mercedes-Benz cars, for example, have a footbrake along the left hand wall of the driver's foot well; this should be depressed to operate, and released using the pull lever on the right hand side. Other vehicles have other methods. In all instances show how the brake operates to avoid panic or mishaps later.

When you leave the car, adjust the seat backwards, leave the gearshift in "neutral" or "park," and remove the key. Retain the key, for safety reasons, until you are back in the car, preferably in the front passenger seat. If you really trust a couple, then let them both sit in the front as they would normally. This will also prove to them that you can be trusted, by trusting them. There is just trust all over the place! The driver will inevitably adjust his seat to his driving position, allowing you to emphasise how easy it is to get comfortable. Once they have changed their mirrors and set themselves up you can proceed. Advise them of the route you plan to take and reassure them that you will direct if they don't know the area.

Now, shut up. Let them ease into the drive and hopefully start getting excited about how the car performs or how safe it feels, whatever is important to them. Don't distract them by hammering on about irrelevant details. They are in control now and want to be stimulated. If they are with their partner then they will converse, usually quietly, and you want to pick up any signs of their first driving impressions. Listen up; valuable knowledge comes at this stage. The more interested in their responses you are the less likely you will be to forget what they liked about the car. There may be questions or concerns about certain items or how the car feels, but remain objective and turn any negatives into positives. For example:

- *"The ride feels a bit harder than ours."*

- "That is because the suspension is set to be firmer which means the car handles better and is more stable through corners – and there's less body roll."

- *"The driving position isn't very comfortable."*

- "Front seats have height, reach and recline adjustment. It might take you a while to fine-tune it but I'm sure, with a bit of tweaking, you will find the driving position very comfortable."

- *"The steering feels a little heavy at speed."*

- "That is because the car has progressive power steering, which gives you light steering when you're parking and manoeuvring, but gets progressively heavier the faster you go. That way you get a much more stable feel at higher speeds."

These statements may seem long winded but they illustrate a positive response while detailing the benefit of the feature they are criticising.

If the spouse wants to drive, halfway back to your premises you can request that the driver pulls in safely and they change over. This will not always be the case, but where there is a spouse it is good practice to offer them a drive, rather than assuming the person driving first is the only decision maker. Where there is a spouse it is essential that you get them on your side, because depending on what type of person they are, they may well have the biggest influence on whether the car meets their requirements against your competition. Often you struggle to build rapport with the primary driver, but you manage to get on famously with their spouse. This shows respect and will build trust extremely quickly with both parties. The behind-the-scenes benefit of this scenario is huge, because unbeknown to you the spouse will convince their partner that you are indeed trustworthy and more importantly that the car is the one for them.

The same goes if your customers are a family. Make every effort to ensure that their children feel comfortable and secure; furthermore making them laugh will earn brownie points with their parents. If you get the spouse to drive the vehicle, the same rules apply. Let them concentrate and enjoy the drive. Don't make conversation and interrupt their thought pattern.

During the demonstration there is one exception to the quiet rule; if the customer has a part-exchange. The following is a common trick of the trade - albeit an old trick - however it can be very useful, depending on your nerve. As the driver makes a turn ask them two questions in quick succession.

1. How long have you had your car?
This is a pre-cursor for the poignant question that follows. It can be useful in determining whether the customer has had value for money for their car or not, i.e. if they haven't had the car very long they will have lost a lot more than they think.

2. How much are you looking to return for it?
Bang. That will hit them like a sledgehammer, especially as they are concentrating on any approaching vehicles as they make their turn. With other things on their mind they are much more likely to answer the question rather than think of a witty response or an inflated figure. Try it. It works. You should decide beforehand, though, whether you want to know their required PX value or not. The downside is that knowing there is a gulf between their expectations and the real value can make you negative when it comes to negotiations.

Once you get back to your place of work you have several options for where you would like them to park. The customer will generally ask you. If at all possible it is recommended that you park next to their own vehicle, if they have one. This is wise, because they will instantly compare old and new.

Pre-Close

Before they get out it is imperative to pre-close the customer. This is done by asking another two decisive questions.

1. Do you like the car? / Is this the car for you?
You need to get confirmation on whether they like the car before anything else. If they don't like it you need to know sooner rather than later. No point getting to the negotiation stage if they don't like the car in the first place!

2. Subject to figures, would you like to buy the car now? / Setting the figures aside, is there anything stopping you from buying the car today?
This is the commitment question. It will clarify whether the customer is serious about buying the car subject to negotiations, and more importantly if they are willing to do business now, today, straight away, not sometime in the future when they have shopped you against the competition.

The pre-close gives the customer the opportunity to tell you if there is anything they are not happy with, such as the colour or the fact that there is no CD player. Whatever the objection is you now have the chance to handle it correctly. Probe further, find out if their objection would stop them purchasing entirely or whether a compromise can be reached.

Leave the car and wait for a few minutes; let them carry on looking and move towards their car. This will encourage them to compare old and new. By building more desire they will not want to keep their old car for long. They are getting the bug now. Remember they have decided to go out looking, visited your showroom, then responded to you which shows real interest, but not necessarily intent. You will have spent about an hour (if you have been doing the job properly) with them so far, so you need to protect your time investment. To progress any further you need to know that their intentions are what you need them to be: to purchase a car and more importantly, the car you have selected, presented and demonstrated to them.

Now, get your customers back to your desk. Don't allow them to wander round looking for a quick exit. Nice one, driven the car now let's get out of here! Entice them with some of that freshly ground instant half caff' peach Melba cappuccino espresso coffee that you have! Just get them seated. Do not let them leave.

Depending on your style and confidence you may wish to sit with them in a less intimidating area rather than at your desk. Somewhere quiet, but comfortable. This should make them feel more relaxed.

Pre-close again before leaving them to await the outcome. Advise them that you are going to see your manager and he will get three independent valuations on their car. The suggestion that the valuations are independent eliminates you from direct responsibility for the amount their car has de-valued during ownership.

Second Management Review

Once you have your victims committed and sat comfortably, trot back to your manager. This is the opportunity to discuss a proposition for the sale of the car. Try to bear in mind that the customer is waiting and is psychologically at their peak in terms of their buying process. The longer you prolong their excitement the less potent it becomes. If you choose to let them leave without a proposal and promise to call them, you are allowing their desire to drop and the rejection will remove any credibility you have established.

Inform your manager of the following:

- Brief customer profile
- Car they are interested in
- Part-exchange appraisal
- Commitment to purchase
- Funding options discussed with the customer

Keep the discussion brief and focus on the information required from your manager:

- Part-exchange valuation
  - Stand in value (SIV)
    - Present
    - Future (if handover is in the future)
- Customer proposal
  - Breakdown of the deal
- Potential movement
  - Comfortable amount of discount permitted to secure a deal

The debate on whether your manager should advise you on the amount of profit in the vehicle will come later. Everyone works differently and there are pros and cons depending on your role within the company. I believe it is important for you to have an idea of it as it will assist you in the negotiation stage which follows.

While you are waiting for the information from your manager you should be preparing for the negotiation. Reconsider what your customer has told you about their requirements and marry this to the vehicle you want to sell them. Also check the details of their car to remind you of any damage or information that reduces its market value. You will need to be armed and dangerous, because you will never offer them more than their car is worth. So, get prepared, get the information from your boss and go get 'em Tiger, before they get too bored and lose interest.

Negotiation

Firstly to ensure that you are fully prepared for the negotiation stage you must be aware of the following products.

GAP (Guaranteed Asset Protection) Insurance

This is an FSA regulated product, normally dealt with by a business manager. If your facility does not have one in place then, as this is an insurance product, you should be FSA regulated to sell it:

- Offer the customer GAP insurance to give them financial security in the event of their new car being written off or stolen and un-recovered.

- Impress on them the fact that they will be given remuneration for the loss between the current market value and the invoice price they paid for the vehicle.

- Make the customer aware that they will be covered for three years.

- Also note that they can pay a one-off fee or take 0% interest over 12 monthly payments (subject to availability).

Paint Protection

This is an interior and exterior protection package, which is guaranteed for at least three years:

- Tell your trusting customer that this product will save them time and energy when cleaning their new purchase.

- Discuss their cleaning methods and emphasise their need to benefit from this effective paint seal.

    o They wash the car, wipe it down with a leather, then there is no necessity for polishing, as the paintwork has been sealed.

- Make sure they are aware of the protective qualities of the product on seats as well as door and roof linings.

    o Any spillages on the fabric can be removed easily.

    o Mention the 3 year guarantee.

12 Month Warranty

This is a policy generally provided to repair or replace specific faulty items:

- Briefly reinforce the benefits of the warranty.

- Choose a part that you know is covered and mention the normal cost to replace that part. Whether the warranty is chargeable or included, reinforce the value of peace of mind.

- Inform the customer of any roadside assistance package that is included within this product.

Extended Warranty

- Tie this product in with all forthcoming MOT tests that may require part replacements that could be covered by this warranty.

- Inform the customer of any roadside assistance package that is included within this product.

Personal Contract Plan (PCP)

The PCP was designed to defer a proportion of the amount funded to the end of the agreement. This reduces the monthly payments and offers the customer three choices at the end of the term:

- The guaranteed minimum future value (GMFV) of the car is determined at the start based on the type of vehicle, length of the agreement and the mileage per annum that the customer estimates.

- The benefit to the customer is that they can finance the car for a lower monthly payment against traditional hire purchase over the same period.

  o Or they can buy the car over a shorter period against traditional hire purchase.

- In a market that is suffering from rapidly declining residual values, this product offers the buyer a guaranteed minimum future value. Not only is the residual value predicted for the end of the term, but also it is secured as a minimum offer, subject to mileage and fair wear & tear. Therefore if the car is worth less than the prediction the car can be handed back and any negative equity is not transferred to the customer.

  o Make the customer aware that if they use hire purchase or borrow from the bank, this guarantee against further loss does not apply.

- At the end of the agreement the customer has three choices:

  1. Pay the GMFV to own the vehicle.

  2. Part-exchange the car. If the offer received for the PX is greater than the GMFV then the customer keeps the change.

  3. Hand the vehicle back to the manufacturer. If the offer received for the PX is less than the GMFV then it is wise to hand the car back to avoid paying the negative equity.

- Some agreements allow the customer to re-finance the GMFV at the end of the term. This allows them to keep the car and pay the deferred sum over an additional period. Check the options available before offering this service.

Negotiation is the most challenging stage so far. All the niceties will go flying out of the window if it is not handled professionally and with tact. You are trying to relieve the buyer of their well earned money and it can get personal. Remember, though, that you are presenting a proposal on behalf of the company - not you personally. You should not be affected by a negative response towards your figures. That's the whole point of a negotiation; it is intended to produce an agreement of terms as the result of a discussion.

The easiest way of presenting a deal is to use a proposal sheet or write-back sheet, where all the necessary figures are itemised and calculated to leave a "price to change". This is the only figure that should matter to you and the customer, as it is the figure they will need to pay to swap their existing car for the new one that they are committed to purchase. It is also the figure that they can compare against any other deals they may have been offered.

Unfortunately customers will, more than likely, use the part-exchange figure to negotiate with, saying that they have been offered more elsewhere or that they are not prepared to let you take the car for that price. It is important for you to convince them that the price to change is the bottom line and move their thoughts away from their PX value. It can be difficult to do this without the aid of a proposal sheet. This eliminates the "back of a fag packet" illegible scribbling that most sales people adopt, which looks wholly unprofessional and offers the customer better leverage. What tends to happen with a quick note of the essential figures is that most of the additional charges (such as road fund licence) are left out. Consequently when they are introduced the customer says they assumed they were included, and will then expect them on top of the discount they require. This puts you on the back foot and widens the financial gap between you.

Apart from the purpose outlined above, the proposal sheet is also essential because it allows you to include any other products or services your company can provide. It gives direction to your presentation of the figures and in most cases, it distracts the customer from their usual objections. Any concessions you may have to offer to secure the deal can be made using ancillary products, rather than profit. It also shows that you and the company you represent are professional and take the negotiations seriously by presenting them in a structured manner, not on a scrap of paper.

The following illustration demonstrates the information required to present your offer successfully:

Customer proposal presented by Scott Owen for Mr Boswell				

Vehicle details	Make	*Aston Martin*	Registration No	*SCO7OWN*
	Model	*DB9*	Registration Date	*01/03/2007*
	Selling price		£21,995.00	Screen price
	Road fund licence		£170.00	6/12 months
	First registration fee		N/A	New cars only

Products	GAP Insurance		£495.00	FSA regulated 36 month cover
	Paint protection		£395.00	36m guarantee for interior and exterior protection
	12 month warranty			Mechanical and electrical warranty
	Extended warranty	*18m*	£850.00	Protects investment for duration of ownership
	Accessories	*Ipod*	£295.00	Dealer fitted equipment
		Roofrack	£350.00	

Part-exchange details	Registration number		*AT04KER*	
	Model		*BMW 320d*	
	Market valuation	1	£6,000.00	Independent valuation of part-exchange vehicle
		2	£5,750.00	Independent valuation of part-exchange vehicle
		3	£6,200.00	Independent valuation of part-exchange vehicle
	Month		*November*	
	PRICE TO CHANGE		**£18,350.00**	FINAL FIGURE REQUIRED FOR PURCHASE
	Security deposit required		£1,000.00	Holding deposit required to secure vehicle

Funding Options	Deposits	PX value	£6,200.00	Market value of PX if used as deposit
		Cash	£2,500.00	Additional cash input, if applicable
	Balance		**£15,850.00**	Balance remaining to be funded

Hire purchase

Term	Payment	Protection		
24	£739.67	None		Unprotected payment over 24 months
36	£519.53	None		Unprotected payment over 36 months
48	£409.46	None		Unprotected payment over 48 months

Personal Contract Plan (PCP), based on 10,000 miles per annum

Term	Payment	Protection	GMFV	
24	£649.00	None	£10,500.00	Unprotected payment over 24 months exc. GMFV
36	£425.00	None	£7,800.00	Unprotected payment over 36 months exc. GMFV
48	£309.00	None	£5,500.00	Unprotected payment over 48 months exc. GMFV

Please note that this proposal is for illustration purposes only and is subject to standard terms and conditions of sale.

The finance figures are purely fictitious; they're designed only to show you the benefits of offering a customer a limited choice.

It is not prudent to over-complicate things as the customer may not have the intelligence or temerity to digest too much information. They will be looking for specific details - primarily the valuation of their car. The whole idea is to present the information relevant to the deal while also prompting you to discuss other products and services that you can provide. All sales people will be measured on their success in meeting targets, in which inevitably accessories are included.

Let's go through the list and take some time to find the best way to present the long awaited figures to your prospective customer, at the height of their curiosity.

Selling Price

Introduce the selling price of the car as they have seen it on display.

If the price has been reduced recently, it gives them an immediate alarm that it will not be reduced substantially more. Make the point that even though they have seen it at this price, they should know it is good value within the market place.

They may agree with you if they have seen it advertised at a higher price. By commenting, you will remind them and the more honest customer will allow you this concession. The fact that it is already cheap should prepare your argument better for later on.

Road Fund Licence

Declare RFL early to avoid conflict and yet another concession at the end of proceedings.

First Registration Fee

This a government tax on all new cars, and it should be itemised to make the customer aware. (This tax does not apply to used vehicles.)

Gap Insurance

State the price for GAP for three year cover, then guard against any questions.

Inform your customer that it is a regulated product and you will discuss that with them later.

Paint Protection

Another product that should be mentioned but not elaborated on.

Advise them that you will demonstrate the product before they leave.

12 Month Warranty

Mention the minimum warranty that your company offers.

The majority will offer 12 month warranty; however the minimum UK requirement is three months.

Extended Warranty

Mention the extended warranty package, in line with the duration your customer intends to keep their car. Then move on.

Accessories

Only discuss accessories if the customer has specifically mentioned a requirement earlier.

Reinforce their need with a price included in your proposal. They will appreciate the fact that you remembered and have got the price for them.

Part-Exchange Valuation

Explain that you have had three market valuations for their car. Say that these estimates are from main dealers or a third party, depending on the type of car:

- State 1st valuation
- State 2nd valuation
- State 3rd valuation

Keep it fluent and straightforward.

Price To Change

This is the important one; make them aware of the price to change.

Then shut up.

After it has hung in the air for a second or two, go on.

Cash Deposit & Payment Terms

Switch them straight into a payment profile:

- State that with their deposit they will pay X amount over 24 months

- State that with their deposit they will pay Y amount over 36 months

- State that with their deposit they will pay Z amount over 48 months

Inform the customer that all the monthly figures quoted exclude insurance. This may prompt them to request a quote for insured payments instead.

Extended Funding Options

Inform your customer that they can benefit from lower payments if their ownership profile suits the PCP method.

Ascertain their annual mileage and ownership period.

You should recommend the PCP funding option if they do average annual mileage and intend to keep their car between 2 and 4 years.

Your Main Aim

The aim is to get through the proposal uninterrupted and un-bruised. This is a mighty task because your customer will react quickly to any elements he disagrees with. Tactfully insist that you are permitted to finish the proposal and then you will be pleased to answer any concerns. Complete the task in a positive manner and then wait for a response.

Tailor your presentation to the customer's preferred method of payment. If their original intention is to pay cash, then finish on the price to change. You can then move on to the funding options once you have completed the deal. If they originally expressed interest in funding with you then go directly to Mayfair. Offer them the monthly payment profile on your proposal sheet.

Inevitably, you will now be moving towards objection handling. This is your opportunity to reveal your real negotiation skills. To handle concerns you need to show empathy, share the concern and emphasise positively why it doesn't present a problem to their purchase. At this point there should not be any problems with the car itself, as you would have committed the customer before negotiating.

The main objection will always be money, even if the price to change is deemed, by them, to be sensible. Personally I would be suspicious if the customer rolled over and went for everything offered at the price offered. Be aware that all may not be as it seems; for example, their part-exchange may have a terminal problem and they are just happy to move it on. Some honest sales people will advise their superiors and recommend the car is inspected prior to completing the deal. However the majority will just bite the customer's generous hand off and sign them up sharpish.

Do not lose focus at this point. This is not the time for the faint hearted.

We are now entering into objection handling as the damned customer has not truly fallen for your smooth talking. Sadly they have rejected your offer and intend to start kicking your arse on price. The negotiation carries on but you will be expected to counter all challenges and remove any concerns that will stop the deal proceeding. Handle the objections carefully, and then close.

Although these elements are all part of the negotiation, we must discuss them separately to appreciate fully the key skills required to turn prospects into customers.

Objection Handling

When handling objections keep an open mind and listen to the customer's true feelings. There are several ways of identifying true intentions.

As you get objections throughout the whole process, you already will have established what type of people the customers are and how they present themselves. Concerns often get voiced unnecessarily because you are being tested on your ability to defend your product or service. If you defer the question until later, the customer will forget to mention it again unless it is a true objection. If this is the case you can overcome it later on and you have had the benefit of foresight, as the customer has forewarned you that this issue concerns him. You can brief yourself prior to the question coming up again. The beauty of this method is that you can move the question on and think about a plausible response if it comes back; if not, then great - you have got rid of another red herring.

Effective listening is more important at this stage than at any other, because the human brain can compute thoughts at least four times faster than it takes for it to receive information. In other words, we can think much more quickly and be several jumps ahead of the information we are processing.

Have you ever had the feeling that you knew what someone was going to say before they said it? Or you knew something was going to happen? That's your mind playing tricks on you. You can use it to your advantage. We all do it, every day. You have an answer to a question in your mind, before the sentence is finished. It's a good trick, so use it wisely.

Be prepared to probe into the customer's objections further. Good questioning will identify a solution to a concern, whether that is to offer a concession or to divert their thoughts to an item they will get that they don't have at the moment.

Use all your body language skills to see if the customer's speech matches their gestures. If it doesn't, this signals a contradiction and suggests the objection is not a major concern. Don't jump in immediately; pause for thought. This will allow you time to answer their query with some thought, rather than ad-libbing, and they will realise that you are listening and thinking about what they are saying - hence taking them seriously. The other advantage of this technique is that quite often the customer will answer their own question, putting their own mind at rest. Brilliant! You didn't even have to say anything. If you had you would have blown the opportunity to let another objection drift away.

If the objection comes in the form of cheaper prices elsewhere, then qualify this. You cannot receive this kind of criticism without making the buyer justify his information. At what prices have they seen alternatives?

They brought the subject up, so they should be responsible for backing their argument up; otherwise they just look like bluffers. What model, year, mileage was the other car? What extras did the other car have? Make notes at this stage which shows them you are taking them seriously. While writing, give yourself time to compare the information given against the car you want them to purchase. If the details they give you seem too good to be true, then they probably are. Oh dear, the customer is lying again.

If they say that the car they have seen is exactly the same as yours, with lower mileage, slightly newer, with bigger wheels and shinier paint then usually they are bluffing. Ask them where the car was being sold from. This may provide valuable information on the source of the cheaper car, giving you an opportunity to question the type and length of warranty cover they may expect or the level of preparation they should expect from your rival. Sow the seeds of doubt. Advise your trusted buyer that you will not offer the cheapest car, but you are very confident you will offer better value for money against the competition. Where the customer is digging his heels in, ask him politely what has stopped them buying that car? You have nothing to lose at this stage if they don't look like they want to budge. It may just be convenience or the colour, in which case you can work on finding some common ground regarding price.

Be proud of your pricing policy and all the products you offer. Never be afraid to offer a cheaper car if you are not getting any movement from the customer. Instead of saying no directly, you are giving the customer a face saver, allowing them to choose an alternative that suits their budget more appropriately. Ha! No, you're not. Well, you are, but deep down you are trying to challenge their ego. This will not work on everyone, so be careful. If you mess with the bull you get the horns. However, the right customer will normally insist he can afford this car and throw in another objection instead. At least you have reinforced that you are not willing to discuss anything unrealistic.

By using the proposal sheet at the start of the negotiation, you will have been discussing a price to change including all other products you offer. Even if the customer has asked for certain items to be removed, you may still have a further item you can remove from the package - or preferably offer a reduced fee for this item - therefore reducing the overall cost and bringing the price closer to their target. This is not necessarily defeatist because you are still protecting the profit you have in the deal. It is a valiant effort to meet their requirements without dumping money and rolling over easily.

Take control and steal their thunder. Go for the kill. Say no, but back it up by offering them reasons for saying no. It is good advice to show them the guide price on their car, if it backs up your argument. In situations where the car you are selling is over age and won't make any profit, show them the stock list detailing how much the car owes the company. Follow this up by putting values to the work you will do to the car, how much VAT you pay and what your bottom line is. Offer proof to your reasons why you are unable to reduce your price any further. Stand firm and close the deal. The timing is perfect for finishing the negotiation at that stage. Even if you offer a final incentive, make it a product that benefits the business. Mats, for example, introduce profit to the business, where as road fund license costs you money. (I'm stating the bleeding obvious now!)

A final method of standing firm is to insist that you are now at your "walk away" point. If their target price means that the deal is not suitable for the business then a deal will not happen anyway, so tell them you are willing to walk away and the final decision is theirs. They now know they will have to spend more to get the car they want. It is a take it or leave it approach, but again it reinforces what they are getting for their money.

Closing The Sale

Do not let them leave. Remember your job is to sell the car. Advise your manager that you have committed your customer to purchase at a certain figure and everything has been done to close the deal on your terms. The decision is now in the hands of the business. It's down to them; let the customer walk, or sell the car now. Even though you may feel the deal cannot be done, it is not up to you. More often than not a final compromise is offered or the deal is sealed on the customer's final demand. Job done. If you get agreement from your manager you have just sold a car and it's a well deserved success. If not, then at least you have done the most you can do and you can move on to the next victim.

There are various different closes that can be used, depending on the subject of the conversation. As with many of the elements of the sales process, the close or at least the trial close is done throughout, by deliberately seeking confirmation from the customer of their desire to purchase the car. As the conversation flows there are plenty of chances to get a trial close in there.

You should adopt the ABC method: always be closing. It sounds cheesy, but the mentality of closing as you go along helps develop a pattern, continuously closing any opportunities for the customer to escape.

Trial Closes

Trial closes are about getting valuable opinions. They can be expressed as an open or closed question, or even as a statement, just as long as the result is some kind of assurance or confirmation. A well-rehearsed sales person will always be pre-closing, making suggestions and getting agreements, all the way through. It is also an open style of questioning which builds rapport. You have continuous opportunities to find out when to close. Listen up and make sure you do not miss the chance to confirm something. Even repeating their sentence can achieve success, because their brain will translate that as confirmation of their stated preference.

Intersperse your natural conversation with direct but well hidden phrases. There are trigger words you can use in your sentences to embed information subconsciously into your customer's mind. We will go into that in more detail later.

Here are a few trial closes that I have heard over the years, although the harshness does vary.

1. "I'm not going to sell you a car today. I'm just going to show you what we can offer you."

2. "How long do you intend to keep the car?"

3. "If we can find you a car in silver would that be more interesting?"

4. "Can you see yourself driving this car?"

5. "Do you really expect us to take your car?"

6. "What don't you like about your current car?"

7. "Shall we go for a drive in your new car?"

8. "Do you want to park it up in the 'sold' row?"

9. "If I could show you the best investment you have ever made, are you in a position to leave a deposit for a car today?"

10. "We generally ask for three colour choices to make sure we don't disappoint. What will yours be?"

11. "I would like your business so I can get my son Max the other shoe that I promised him."

12. "Setting the figures aside, is there anything stopping you from buying the car now?"

13. "You prefer the silver car with the leather interior? Good, I'm pleased."

14. "How important to you are service and preparation?"

15. "In your opinion, which car most suits your needs?"

16. "Do you feel we could do a deal today?"

17. "If we can get your car ready for the weekend, would you consider buying it now?"

18. "I can see you're eager to get it; we'd best go and sort the deal out for you."

Close

Now for the close - the killer finish at the end of a lengthy, but thorough presentation of your product and services. Congratulate yourself for getting this far. But don't get the Krug out just yet.

This is what you have been working towards and you can almost smell it (the sale, that is). It's dead simple. Draw the customers in by leaning towards them a bit, as if to show them you are telling them something you don't want anyone else to know. They will mirror your gesture, I almost guarantee it. Watch the personal space though; you don't want to receive a whiff of their breakfast. Horrific breath can devastate you just as your about to close the sale. You will be coughing and wheezing like an asthmatic coal miner.

So lean in, wait for them to respond, then hit them with your close. It should be a one liner, not too dressed up, just a concise professional sentence that rolls off your tongue. There are many approaches, so you need to find a few that you feel most comfortable with. Once you have secured the deal, always shake the customers' hands and I mean all of them. Even if they have children, shake theirs too; it usually makes them laugh. Remember, you're a family friend now! Well OK, perhaps I shouldn't go that far.

Here are a few examples of relevant closing methods which have been tried and tested by professional sales people. Some are more complex than others:

Alternative Close

Offer a choice of two or three options, whether that is the car itself (more likely to be on a new model) or a choice of package. You can offer the customer two or three price to change options, thereby forcing them to choose a preference. The ball is in their court and more often than not they will choose the middle option, not wanting to appear cheap while minding their budget.

- "Would you prefer the silver or black car?"

    o *"The silver / black car."*

        - "Do we have your business on the terms discussed?" or

        - "You have just bought yourself a car, thanks for your business."

- "Which price option suits you best?"

    o *"We prefer the second one. We like the Supagard but we're not too bothered about the GAP."*

        - "OK brilliant, I know what you're saying about the GAP, but we are duty bound to discuss it with you as it is an important product, but let's do the paperwork first." or

        - "That's great. The paperwork will only take ten minutes. Can I get you another drink?"

Assumptive Close

This is one of the best, due to the fact you are already positive and confident and are getting along famously with your customers. Assume they are purchasing regardless of the minor details and keep repeating their confirmations of preference. That old mind trick again. Try to refrain from being cocky and overwhelming; play it down. There is a fine line between confidence and arrogance.

- "So, when would you like to take delivery?"
    - *"Before the weekend would be ideal."*
        - "I will check with our service department, but I'm sure that should be OK."
    - *"How long do you think it will take?"*
        - "Once we've taken your deposit we normally allow for three days."
- Get your order form out and say: "How do you intend to pay the deposit? Debit or Credit Card?"
    - *"Uurrrggghhh, we have cash for the deposit."*
        - "OK, excellent. Let me get you a coffee while we complete the deal."
    - *"Can we pay by Switch?"*
        - "Yes, that's fine."

Best Time Close

The "best time to buy" can be off-putting, almost testing the customer's resolve. It can, however, be very effective with the right people. Tell them of a poignant moment when you didn't purchase an item you craved only to find they had sold out when you did go back.

- "My colleague has just taken a call on that car."

    o *"Oh right. Well we would like to buy it, what do we need to do?"*

        ▪ "All you need to do is sign the paperwork and leave a deposit. We will do the rest."

    o *"We were here first so we will take it."*

        ▪ "Brilliant, it's yours then. We don't want any squabbling!" Laugh.

- "It's close to your birthday I see; look at it as your treat."

    o "Very observant, yes it is, but don't mention my age."

        ▪ "I won't mention your age if we have a deal."

    o "Okay, I think we will have it, thanks."

        ▪ "Excellent, the rest won't take long and many happy returns for next week."

Distraction Close

If it feels like you're banging your head against a wall because the customer has a hesitant or analytical mindset, you may decide to distract them before stealing in there with a straightforward close. This can be done subtly by introducing them to the service or parts department, or showing them round the car again. The idea is to catch them off guard by talking about something else, before eliciting a positive response from them.

- "I thoroughly recommend that you consider investing in the car while you're here, but while you're thinking about it I will introduce you to the service department."

    o *"OK, thanks."*

        ▪ Make the final close in front of your service colleague by saying: "Shall we go complete the paperwork?"

        ▪ Or take advantage if their phone goes off. Just before they answer it, put your hand out and close: "Let's complete the paperwork."

Red Faced Close

This is the chance to shame your customer into submission, especially if they have been particularly rude to you. Every dog has his day and now you can make them feel embarrassed not to buy. The two basic ways of doing this are either to flatter them by playing up to their ego, or by suggesting they would be left with egg on their face if they don't buy. This can be accomplished with either sex, but it is a high risk manoeuvre. Blow this and you can risk the whole deal for an over-friendly comment. It works best with affluent types who like to keep up with the Joneses. While they have been lording it, acting like the cock o' the north, they will be side-swiped when you test their pride.

- "Bet you don't want to go home in your old car, now do you?"
  - *"Not at all, it's been a good car, still is."*
    - "We can have your new one ready for the weekend if we agree the deal now."
      - *"Okay, that sounds good."*
- "This car will be the pinnacle of your motoring experience."
  - *"We have had some good cars, but we have always wanted a (brand)."*
    - "Let's do the deal then."

Nodding Dog Close

This is a good way of closing the amiable customer. In a situation where you have been getting positive feedback throughout the process, you can take advantage of their need to agree with people by summarising the points of your proposal. Your buyer will automatically nod or say yes to carefully selected closed questions about what they are buying, selling to you, how they are paying, any items included within the deal and the price to change. Another good tip is to have a checklist in front of you and make a point of ticking the points as you ask them, hence encouraging the customer even more to agree with you. It also lets you know if there are any last minute objections. If there are, you can handle them swiftly, gain agreement and carry on through your list.

- "I would just like to take a moment to go through everything."

- "Correct me if I'm wrong, but I feel we have selected the right car."

- "Yes."

- "We have inspected your car in its present condition."

- "Yes."

- "We have presented the figures and agreed a suitable compromise."

- "Yes."

- "Then can I have your business?"

- "Yes."

Last Chance Close

The "last chance" is exactly what it says on the tin and should only be used if you have exhausted all other options and the customer is walking away to consider the deal. It may appear desperate and it is, but it could just clinch the deal for you, which is why it is essential as a final attempt. There is nothing to lose because they are leaving anyway, but there is everything to gain which is all you deserve after spending time assessing their needs.

- "Is there anything we can do to get your business now?"

- *"Yes, if you give us another £1,000."*

- "We can't do that but what if I can prove to you that you will get that £1,000 back when you change your car next time?"

- *"OK, convince me and we have a deal."*

I'm sure you and your manager can come up with sound evidence to show the extra £1,000 you are asking for will result in a better residual value. It's simple; if you can prove it then you have a deal with a customer who was willing to walk.

Ultimatum Close

By introducing an ultimatum you are confirming that this deal will not be available beyond this point. It is a very common close, even used regularly in TV advertising. A typical example is the DFS Sale, "but remember it ends on Sunday." Then another one begins. In your case there are several believable ways to suggest this deal will not be here tomorrow. For example, you could say that there is a limited number of vehicles left and with the amount of advertising the company does we are receiving plenty of phone calls on this exclusive offer. If that is too long winded then make it concise and credible.

- "My advice is to secure the deal today to avoid disappointment."

- *"You're bound to say that though. I think it's best for me to let you know tomorrow."*

- "I know how you feel, a lot of my customers have felt the same way, but after realising that it would save time the next day, they found it easier to complete the paperwork there and then."

- *"Yes, I suppose they are right."*

The "Only" Close

This is more of a technical close. If there is a gulf between you and the customer after you have presented your proposal then you can break the difference down. Rather than seeing it as a big chunk of money, relate it in terms of annual, monthly and weekly multiples. This makes their appeal less effective and again plays on their pride when it's only X amount a month above their budget. If there is more than one decision maker include them both in the discussion. Not only is this polite but also it encourages decisive action between them, as one will feel more confident than the other and will transfer this confidence on your behalf, thereby convincing the partner to commit. Let them do their own heads in; stand back and watch them argue. My money is on the female.

- "Can we have your business?"

- *"Well if you can reduce the amount by £1,500, then yes we will think about it."*

- "£1,500, wow. That's a big difference. Having said that, if you break it down its only £500 a year, about £41 a month or less than £10 a week."

- *"Fair point, let's do the deal now."*

Guilt Close

Yes, you guessed it, make the beggars feel guilty. The guilt close is a more cynical version of the sympathy close, which people use regularly to varying degrees of success. The idea is to generate as much guilt as possible by repeating what you have done for them and making them feel bad for not giving you the order. This method can work wonders if you get the sympathy flowing gradually, but without aggression. That would just push them out of the door, thinking that you have been their friend who suddenly spits his dummy out because they said no. All too often sales people tend to revert to child mode and suddenly become aloof and awkward. Instead you should concentrate on pro-actively playing the guilt card rather than reactively behaving like a spoilt kid.

- "Shall we go ahead then?"

- *"No, we are going to think about it for a few days."*

- "Oh, that's a shame."

- *"Why's that?"*

- "Well I feel that I have done all I can to help you purchase the right car. I thought we had got the best deal possible from my manager, which wasn't easy and now I feel like I have let you down."

- *"No, not at all, we appreciate what you have done; it's just that we always think things through before deciding."*

- "I apologise if I have missed something that's important to you."

- *"You haven't; it is as simple as I've said, we just need to talk it through."*

- "I tell you what, let me leave you to finalise your decision for 10 minutes while I have a chat with my manager, to see if there is anything else we can do to help you." Then walk off.

You may find that when you return your customer has decided to purchase now rather than wait a few days. Mission accomplished. If not, then at least you have done as much as you can.

Putting It All Together

Hopefully my selection of closes will help the sales person find a comfortable and flowing way of determining whether the customer is pulling their leg or actually intends to purchase. I hope that it will also give the customer an insight into how the closing process works. I'm sure there will be a few people who now realise how they were closed the last time they bought a car, or anything else for that matter. These methods are used in all areas of sales and there are plenty more, most of which do not apply to car sales.

As usual, it all sounds great when it's written down; but if you don't learn these key skills you will never know whether you could have saved the deal. The customer may return or call up to complete the deal, but don't count on it. The chances of a sale after the customer has left are slim to say the least. Why take the chance of leaving them to consider your proposal and be talked out of it by their friends and families, when you have not exhausted every other option available to you? This is where the majority of these closes work most effectively; as a last throw of the dice. Remember closes are not mutually exclusive; they can be combined and repeated in any order you desire. Just do whatever it takes to finalise the deal.

Here now is an example of the general negotiation path following your presentation, through objection handling and closing the sale.

Sales Person:	[Mr/Mrs/Ms _____], we know we have the right car for you and the price to change is £15,850.00. Can we have your business?
Customer:	*Well no, not at that price.*
Sales Person:	OK, let's discuss it.
	We have the right car for you.
	We have got the highest valuation for your car.
	And everything is included to protect your investment.
	What price to change did you have in mind?
Customer:	*I would like something off the car as I'm paying cash.*
Sales Person:	We are not permitted to offer any incentive either way, whether you pay in cash or with finance.

Customer:	*Well, I have seen them advertised cheaper elsewhere and I know my car is worth a lot more than that.*
Sales Person:	As a business we can only offer the amount we can get back for your car. Anything we agree above that figure comes from the profit in our car. So the easiest way is to discuss the price to change.
	That is the bottom line, the amount you pay.
Customer:	*Yes, that's all I'm interested in really.*
	But I think your car is £1000 too much and my car is worth at least £500 more than what you offered.
Sales Person:	We feel our car is priced very competitively in the market place, but we do have a small amount of profit we are happy to share with you.
	But I am nowhere near £1500 off; we don't carry that kind of profit in our cars.
Customer:	*Well, what could you do?*
Sales Person:	If I could just have a minute to reiterate our package.
	Our car comes with a warranty package, roadside assistance and thorough mechanical check.

	We will also replace any tyres under 3mm, make good any paint defects or car park dents and valet the car to the highest standard.
Customer:	*I appreciate that but I am not prepared to pay any more than £15,000.*
Sales Person:	OK. We are at £15,850 plus your car and you want to be at £15,000, is that right?
Customer:	*Yes.*
Sales Person:	OK, I will discuss it with my manager.
	And if we agree to £15,000 you will buy the car now?
Customer:	*Yes.*
Sales Person:	Great, just give me a few minutes to see how close we can get.
	He gets up, turns away, then stops and turns back. He draws breath through his teeth, a favourite technique known as the 'wince' and then says...
Sales Person:	I know I am going to struggle because it's just been reduced. Would you be prepared to do a deal at £15,500?

Customer:	*Well I'm not sure about that. See what your manager says.*
Sales Person:	OK, I will see how far I can push him.
	He sets off to see his manager. An argument ensues, which the customer can hear. They can't determine what is being said but know there are raised voices. He returns five minutes later looking wounded.
Sales Person:	"I couldn't quite get to £15,000, but we would like your business at £15,500."
	He swiftly sticks out his hand to close the deal. Brave move, but he knows he has built enough trust.
Customer:	*Sorry no, I will buy it for £15,250.00, otherwise I'm going home.*
Sales Person:	I can't do it, not with everything we allow for on preparation. Our preference is to make the car right rather than costing you money in the long run.
	Can I have your business if I throw in a set of mats?
Customer:	*OK, let's do the deal.*

Dealt! That was easy!

OK, that is euphoria as far as the negotiation goes. It is difficult to touch on every scenario, but that example is a snapshot of what normally happens. The customer is reluctant to agree too easily, he is trying to spend the least amount possible. The sales person is trying to retain as much profit as they can, as well as retaining vital profit-making and target-achieving add-ons. It is important to reject as many advances for discount as you can, which you do successfully by reverting back to your product and describing items that have already saved the customer money. This way you are not backing down to demands, and are therefore saying no to the customer. Now they realise that you are willing to say no it will diminish their requests. You have also shown them additional value for money and that will justify to them that the purchase is sensible, making them less likely to think they are being ripped off. Each time the customer asks for some form of concession and wins, they become braver. If you back down each time you will appear desperate and the advantage is theirs. They gain control and go for the kill, nicking as much off you as they can. It's all a game. Do not let them do it.

Confirmation & Documentation

Before you complete the paperwork, ask the customer how they intend to pay for the vehicle. Do they want to take advantage of the funding options available? You should know whether you are FSA regulated. If not, then a business manager would take responsibility for the finance and insurance products. "What's one of them?" I hear you say! I will come on to him or her later.

You need to be aware of the documentation you have to complete to satisfy the customer and your business. Everything should be tied down. All decent businesses will have the following documentation, to protect their interests.

Order Form

This is a basic document that displays customer information, along with all the details of the vehicle and the figures agreed between both parties.

Include all accessories that you have agreed within the deal.

If it is a new car, detail all the factory options on the vehicle.

You need to know all elements of VAT to operate efficiently in the UK sector. The Value Added Tax has to be detailed separately and any options or accessories that apply need to be shown exclusive of VAT.

Itemise the price to change, deposit, PX value, amount to be financed (if applicable) and the cash balance to pay on delivery.

Get the document signed and dated by the customer.

Give them their copy of the order form and show them your Terms & Conditions (usually on the back of their copy).

Part-Exchange Declaration Form

The PX declaration confirms all the details given by the customer about their car. If they have told you something and you haven't confirmed anything different from the information you have received about their car, then write it down. If it turns out to be incorrect later, then your company may have some recourse for changing the figures based on the original information offered. In a lot of instances this declaration is included within the order form. Check to see if you need to use a different form.

You need to get the customer to sign this document without fail, preferably on purchase, although there will be exceptions in which case they must sign upon delivery.

Deposit Receipt

All deposits have to be accounted for. Issue a signed receipt to the customer for the initial deposit, normally £1,000 depending on company policy.

Pass the receipt on through the normal channels, usually signed for by the accounts department.

Handover Reminder

Not a common practice but all sales people should offer each customer a handover reminder, which confirms the following details:

- Vehicle details, for insurance information
- Proposed handover date and time
- Part-exchange documents required
- Cash balance (not to exceed £9000, including deposit, on the authority of the FSA)
- Finance balance
- Copy of documents required by the finance department
- Sales person contact details

It's as simple as that. Well, without wishing to bore you, it isn't. Paperwork can become the bane of a sales person's life. As you will spend at least twenty percent of your time completing some form of administration, you should be well versed in all areas to eliminate unnecessary repetition.

The other aspect of being document literate is that your customer will be monitoring your ability to work the figures out and will be looking for a way to contradict your sums. If you're not up to it, then get someone in who can complete everything quickly and accurately. Personally I would make sure I knew how it all worked, to avoid looking thick in front of the customer as well as my colleagues.

Business Manager Role

Although a growing number of dealers now employ a business manager, many do not. For this reason I decided to demonstrate the sales process as though the sales person deals with all aspects of the transaction. It is important to know the whole process without diluting it by separating off the parts which otherwise would be covered by the business manager.

The business manager is responsible for all areas of finance and insurance, along with any money handling. It will be your responsibility to introduce your customer to them, when relevant. Not if, but when. There is no escape for the customer in the 21st century. Failure to comply generally results in a disciplinary, or at least a heated, lecture. By the time your superiors have finished you will feel like you have been in the ring with Ricky Hatton. You have been warned.

An important part of the sales process now is the involvement of the Financial Services Authority (FSA). They regulate the finance and insurance products sold by certified dealerships and dictate a structured way of informing customers, based on best advice.

You will have to inform your customer that the dealership is regulated by the FSA. This usually comes in the form of delivering a statement, advising them that you intend to offer best advice, in accordance with FSA guidelines. It is wise to make this statement early on, at the point of data capture. You will be required to issue an initial disclosure document at the same time. This details your company's procedure with regard to FSA regulations and often gets forgotten by sales people. However if you are "mystery shopped" by the FSA the company will face severe reprimands, including losing the licence required to sell F&I products.

The timing of your introduction depends on how the sale is flowing. Generally the first management review is an ideal place to start a discussion with your BM, as you will be talking through the deal with your sales manager anyway. Kill two birds with one stone and involve them then. Inform them of what information you have gained about F&I and ask them when they want to be introduced. The majority of the time they will not seek to meet the customer until the end, during the negotiation stages.

Advising the customer depends on their intentions, which you will know by the time you get to the first management review stage. You get another bite of the cherry at the second management review. Whatever the circumstances, you must inform your business manager of your progress at this stage, whether it is good news or not. They have to have an opportunity to convert the cash customer or close the finance customer.

Try to get the customer into the BM's office. This is a better environment in which to discuss financial matters, as it offers more privacy. I firmly believe the sales person should stay with the customer while are they are conversing with the BM. This view is not shared by everyone; some people feel that it is the BM's job so let them get on with it. For the sales person, the advantage is that they do not necessarily need to close the deal. The sales person can also use the time to deal with another customer. Although I see their point I believe that the benefits of remaining with your customer far outweigh any benefits of leaving them.

There are incredible benefits to this system, which is why it is common place:

- It gives the sales person back up; a second face to discuss the deal with the customer, who might tell someone else why he is concerned, where he couldn't tell the sales person directly.
- It gives the customer the illusion that the company is thoroughly professional and takes the delicate job of people's finances seriously.
- It also means the customer cannot squirm out of it. If you are telling them it is a requirement of the business that they see your business manager then they have no option.
- If you are present in this meeting you have the added benefit of:
  - Continuation of trust and rapport building with the buyer.
  - Tag team strategy with your BM. You can confirm what each other is saying and reinforce the major points of funding and insurance products.
  - Your BM will qualify the customer's desire to purchase and commit them all over again.
  - The customer is less likely to repeat any objections that you have already handled. If you are not present they may decide to use you as an excuse to walk away from the deal.

Cash Customer

- "I will introduce you to our business manager, who will discuss certain products which are regulated by the Financial Services Authority."

  o *"It's OK, we don't need the finance. We will just pay for it, thanks."*

    ▪ "We can show you the cost of using your own money, but whichever way our business manager will go through the options for paying the balance."

    ▪ Or "That's fine, but we are obliged to ensure we have given you best advice. I will just make sure he is free for you. I won't keep you long."

Finance Customer

- "I will introduce you to my business manager, so you can discuss all your finance options."

  o *"OK, thanks."*

It should not be hard to get your customer into the BM's office. Act as if it is mandatory. They need to be aware that they can save even more money by making a clever purchase. Funding options should be paramount to their buying experience. There are several ways to illicit a need to save their hard-earned money and take advantage of any finance incentives your BM may be aware of.

Another element of the BM's position is to grade the referral from the sales person. Most franchised dealerships operate this system to gain information on a range of customer and employee behaviour. The benefit of grading the sales person's referral to the business manager is that it generates focus, on an individual, to represent the interests of their employer.

F&I are very important to modern dealer groups because they have become one of the most lucrative areas of the business. Only a few years ago, one of the world's largest manufacturers lost $1 billion on the sale of motor vehicles, but made $2 billion from vehicle financing. What does that tell you? It tells me they might as well be a bank; willing to lose on the sale of goods to recoup twice the difference from loaning funds. Why not? Who's the mug?

Back to the grading system. The idea is to ensure that all customers are referred to the BM and that they have an opportunity to offer additional services. Once that process is complete, either in person or by telephone, then the BM is responsible. They will mark you as follows:

- **A:** Referred in person, on the premises
- **B:** Appointment made for BM (within 50 mile radius) or re-appointment
- **C:** Telephone appointment made for BM (outside 50 mile radius)
- **D:** Telephone appointment made for BM (within 50 mile radius)
- **X:** No referral made

The system is straightforward enough, even though it appears that you are being judged. It is more about finding out how many customers are being seen at the best opportunity and how successful the BM is, compared with telephone appointments.

The X referral does incite a feeling that it may not be the best idea to get one, and that is exactly right. As with a lot of processes that are put in place by your superiors, this one comes with an "if you blow it" clause. The dreaded X referral means that you will lose sales commission on this deal, and in many cases all deals done within that month. Not just the finance commission but the money earned from the sale of the car also. Yikes… whether they carry it through or not, you will end up in the middle of a shit storm if you are given an X.

Buying Signals

Open your eyes and ears. It's alright going on about the sales process, but if you miss vital buying signals you can forget selling the car on the day.

You can miss an early sale if you fail to acknowledge and act upon a specific desire to purchase upon a condition. We have already mentioned ten closes, so now let's elaborate on the buying signals that you need to be aware of. I also give you an example of a response which will capture the moment and confirm an intention to purchase.

"Not sure about the colour. Do they do it in black?"

a) "If I could get a black one would you consider buying it?"

b) "That is the only one remaining at that price, would the colour stop you from buying it?

"I'm not familiar with automatic. Can you get me a manual?"

a) "Have you ever felt the benefits of an automatic gearbox?"

b) "If we could get you a manual would you be prepared to buy it, subject to test drive?"

"I am not sure if we should let our car go for that price."

a) "I can understand that, but I don't think you will get more unless you sell it privately and that can be a gamble."

b) "You could keep it for that price and let someone in the family inherit it; call it an early Christmas present."

"What do think our car is worth, just an as idea?"

a) "We can look at the value of your car, but if we get the right price will you buy a car off us today?"

b) "We do have a valuation service, where you pay £50 for us to value your car independently."

    o *"What, you mean we have to pay to get our car valued?"*

        ▪ "Sorry, no, I mean we offer it as part of the service if you want to change your vehicle. If not, we charge £50 to value your car independently."

"Do you have credit facilities?"

a) "Yes, we have a business manager who can discuss what's best for you."

b) "We do, yes. How long is your preferred term and how much would you like to pay per month?"

"Are there any with leather? We saw an Audi we liked that had it."

- "Would you like leather? We can get it fitted."

- *"We would consider it, depending on price."*

- "Shall we include it within the price of this exchange?"

- *"No, leave it out for now."*

"Do we have to buy it if we drive it?"

a) "I would like to think you would want to buy it once you have driven it."

b) "Well I cannot guarantee you won't, that's up to you, I just know you will like the car."

"How much is a service?"

- "We have a maintenance charter which means the prices are fixed within the network. I'll introduce you to our service department after we have agreed the figures."

"Did you sell a car to John Randell?"

- "Yes I did? Nice guy. Did he tell you the deal he got?"

- *"He might have mentioned it."*

- "I bet you want the same deal, don't you?"

- *"Well, I would like to trump him with a better deal really."*

- "That's a tough call, but if we beat his deal for you, can we have your business today?"

"We can't really do anything until we return from holiday."

- "Would you buy it now if we can have it on your drive for when you return?"

The aforementioned statements may appear to be no more than the usual pre-close or close, and guess what? They are. However, they are examples of how you need to spot positive clues and commit them to purchase. This can be done more subtly by toning down your response, gently moving them forward in the process, rather than using an outright close. Whichever method you use, make sure you don't miss the opportunity. Success in spotting buying signals is achieved by clever direction of a customer's intention and interest in purchasing your product.

No matter how slight you think their feeling of desire is, it must be brought to the fore. Explore every avenue that the customer opens up and devour their need for confirmation. This reduces their reasons for saying no at a later stage. When they contradict a previous point they made in the conversation, a swift reminder to your buyer dismisses their reasoning and negates their argument.

Having said that, try to refrain from being insulting. We are still trying to be friends with the customer and if you piss him off now over a discussion of no consequence, you will feel the heat and find yourself opening the door for them. Remember the customer is king! And they do have the right to be treated in a civilised manner.

Do not miss any buying signals.

Telephone Appointments

Telephone sales enquiries into the dealership or workplace are a valuable source of income. I believe they are just as important as a customer walking in, if they are dealt with correctly. All incoming telephone sales calls should be responded to quickly, in a well rehearsed manner. The easiest way is to use a script. This is nothing new, I can hear you say and you're right; scripts have been around for years and have been used for all sorts of purposes. The common theme is that they are successful at gaining a firm appointment, which is the whole idea. While allowing you to take control, they also remind you to ask the relevant questions, rather than droning on about the information the customer needs.

First you need to qualify the call; whether it is a sales call, a request for an insurance valuation, or a service enquiry. Eliminate anything other than the real thing, with the intention to:

- Gain information on a required car
- Book a test drive
- Value a part-exchange

Your goal is to get them in front of you. By using a ten step telephone script, the caller will be guided through a process, delivering them to your doorstep. This example assumes the call is a qualified sales lead.

Ring ring...

Sales Person:	Good [morning/afternoon], Seegfreed speaking.
Customer:	*Hi, I would like to book a test drive in a 308 please.*
Sales Person:	Would that be petrol or diesel?
Customer:	*Petrol.*
Sales Person:	Are you looking for new or used?
Customer:	*Probably used.*
Sales Person:	I'm just going to check my stock list. Are you calling from home or work?
Customer:	*Home.*
Sales Person:	And the number there is?
Customer:	*Uurrmm, 01472 194738*
Sales Person:	Your name is?
Customer:	*Brian Davidson.*
Sales Person:	One moment, someone is passing me a list; I will check it quickly for you.
	Put the call on hold for a minute.
Sales Person:	We do have a vehicle you can test drive. Which day would you prefer? Thursday or Friday?
Customer:	*Can I come this afternoon?*

Sales Person:	Yes, I will be free after 2pm and we close at 6pm.
Customer:	*We can be there for 3 o'clock.*
Sales Person:	OK Mr Davidson. I'm Seegfreed and I will set that time aside for you, 3pm today. Please bring your driving licences with you; I assume you are both coming?
Customer:	*Yes we are and I will get my licence, see you then, thanks.*

Sounds easy, doesn't it? However awkward the caller gets try to keep them on the script. It will reveal itself in the end. You may need to answer the odd question here and there but the plan is to ask two or three questions about their car of interest, to narrow the options down a bit, as if you are going to find a suitable car to drive.

Then turn the conversation round by asking if they are at home or work. This will give them the impression you are going to call back when you have checked the car's availability for them. The real benefit of the interruption is that you can then move straight into asking their phone number, which is vitally important. No telephone call should be terminated before you have their contact details. Once you have their number, which they usually spit out because you have caught them off guard, then ask their name. People are used to being asked their name first, then their number, in which case they get ample time to consider whether to give their number or not.

If the caller does not wish to give their number, then say you're going to check their vehicle of choice is available for demonstration purposes, and that you will to call them back straight away. Remember this is only a ploy to get their number, so think on your feet and get it. Follow this up with an excuse to hold the line for a moment as the information you need has just been brought to you. This will negate the need to call them back after all. By holding the call for a minute you can make sure you have a car available. If you haven't, just tell them to come in anyway. You can always make an excuse for the car's absence later and test drive them in a suitable alternative.

This system offers a straightforward approach to achieving an appointment from a telephone enquiry. If it does not succeed then what are the customer's actual intentions? If they don't want to give you their number, then how will you be permitted to let them drive one of your cars, as those details will be required when they visit?

Try it. It will save you time, effort and trouble, listening to them drone on about their car and all its history, the fact that it has never been sat in, in the back, or that it has been polished every Sunday. We are not interested in their life story, we just want them to come in and buy a car.

Administration

Once the sale has been completed it is essential that you process all administration quickly and efficiently. I mentioned earlier the importance of completing the necessary paperwork and understanding all elements required, but that is only the start. Once the customer has left, you will need to ensure that all parties concerned know what is going on. It is worth compiling a checklist to remind yourself and other departments of the details they need to prepare the car to the standards required for a smooth handover.

The more quickly you process the information the better chance you will have of catching any problems early enough for them to be resolved in time. This saves you running round like a madman on the day of delivery, just as the customer is walking in expecting everything to be ready. The buck stops with the sales person, regardless of who hasn't done what is required, so make sure you check, double check and triple check, on a daily basis, that the preparation is all in hand.

The administration required following the sale of a vehicle can be split up into the seven departments involved, as follows...

Finance & Insurance Department

- Issue copies of all paperwork relevant to the sale.
- Inform the business manager of any information you have gained from the customer after the sale was concluded.
- Discuss the results of the sale and how it affects the F&I department.
- Take note of the following information, to be included within your record of deals (detailed later in this section):
  - Finance type
  - Amount financed
  - Period of agreement (months)
  - Payment
  - GMFV (if applicable)
  - Deposit (PX value + cash)
  - Referral grade (This is the referral grading system used by some dealerships)
- Request signature and stamped approval of the order form, with the relevant grading box ticked.

Service Department

- Complete a preparation order form.
- Detail all work required.
- Tell a trusted service colleague what your requirements are.
- Gain confirmation of when work can be carried out.
- Issue service order.
- Make a note of who received your request and what date they committed to.

Sales Manager

- Get signatures on part-exchange valuation, order form and deal folder (containing all documents relevant to the vehicle.)
- Issue copy of part-exchange valuation and order form.
- Advise details of vehicle sold, additional items sold and finance agreed.
- Enter deal in delivery diary or on board.
- Request estimate on profit remaining on the car sold. Make a record of this figure.
- Put your sale on the board.
- Congratulate yourself.

Sales Administrator

- Issue all signed documents.
- Advise insurance arrangements.
- Ensure handover date is advised and put in diary.
- Request order to service department to advise:
  - Vehicle preparation required
  - Customer contact details
- Request order to parts department to advise:
  - Accessories required
  - Customer contact details
- Ensure all the following documents and items are in place:
  - Registration document
  - MOT certificate (if applicable)
  - Spare key(s)
  - Original insurance document
  - Signed certificate of entitlement, for cherished number plate (if applicable)

     ○ Signed transfer/retention document (if applicable)

     ○ Cheque for either £80 or £105, depending on transfer or retention (if applicable)

Parts Department

- Copy or separate preparation order.
    - ○ Check items detailed are correct.
- Tell a trusted parts colleague what your requirements are.
- Gain confirmation of the items required.
- Issue parts' copy of preparation order.
- Issue valeter's copy of preparation order.

Customer Relationship Management Department (CRM)

- Complete the order form on your PC, ensuring all details are correct. This will be the information used for the order form.
- Check all figures add up; the customer will receive a copy for their or their accountant's records.
- Ensure customer details are correct; they will be used by the CRM team to follow your customer up after delivery.
- Inform CRM team if there have been any specific requirements from your customer – e.g. they will be on holiday for two weeks, or they prefer not to be called at work.
- Complete all necessary booklets or documents that need to be passed on.

Make it easy for yourself and the customer. Clever and efficient paperwork and concise communication with the relevant parties will alleviate any headaches on handover. Everyone makes mistakes; that's inevitable. However if you have prepared well and then made sure at regular intervals that the necessary work is being processed, you will limit any damage. You will also catch delays early enough to build in concessions or alternatives should you need to. If all else fails, keep the customer informed if you fear the car will not be ready in time. Do not let it get to the day before handover when you tell them any bad news.

Handover Process

For a customer, there is very little better than going to collect your new (or new to you) vehicle from a dealership. The experience can be rated alongside picking up the keys to a new house or flying out on holiday. As you approach and enter the dealership, your excitement builds up; you have finally got here. Only the calmest of people or those who regularly change their car would not feel excitement at this stage. It is a very liberating experience; a chance to try everything out, to get comfortable, personalise your new toy, then give it a blast, feel the different ride quality, build quality, the way the accelerator feels. You can't wait to get going and drive off to enjoy that lunch you promised your wife, or vice versa.

So the last thing you need is some poncey sales person screwing things up for you, making excuses about why this and that hasn't been done. They have had plenty of time. Nothing had better go wrong.

As a salesperson you need to remember this. The perception of the customer will vary from one person to the next at the handover stage, but the crux of the matter will always be two-fold. As described above the expectation level is heightened and the customers will feel elated and excited about the process. So make them feel relaxed and at ease. By presenting yourself calmly and professionally you naturally will exude confidence that everything is in place. Get them comfortable and ready to sign plenty of paperwork.

It is generally a good idea to have the vehicle ready and isolated from the others, ideally in the showroom, or at least outside, in its own space. Try to avoid a long period where the customer is poring over the vehicle and not sitting down signing away. They'll have plenty of time later to get to know the vehicle. Be prepared for the fussy one! I don't mean this offensively (well maybe I do) but some customers can pick flaws invisible to the human eye.

To complete a successful handover you need to work steadily and efficiently. Talk your customers briefly through each document and then ask them to sign both copies, of which they will be given one. It is all too easy to become distracted by persistent questions. Keep focused on the job in hand and advise the customer that you will present the car fully once you have completed the laborious task of finalising clerical matters.

All the following points need to be discussed:

- Documentation in duplicate which requires both parties to sign; issue copy to customer, retain copy for company:
  o Final order form
  o Customer invoice
  o Part-exchange disclaimer
  o Paint protection certificate (if applicable)
- Items not requiring a signature that have to be issued to the customer:
  o Take payment for any outstanding balance and issue receipt for balance paid (if applicable)
  o Supplementary invoice, for additional items
  o MOT certificate

- o Green slip from registration document (the main document has been sent to DVLA)
- o Warranty confirmation and booklet
- o Vehicle handbook, service book, etc...
- o Locking wheel nut remover
- o Spare key(s)
- o Paint protection pack (if applicable)
- o Cherished number DVLA receipt (if applicable)
- o Accessories, such as:
  - Telephone cradle
  - Child car seat
  - Toys, pens, clothing, etc...
- CSI questionnaire (Customer Satisfaction Index)
  - o Inform your customers that the manufacturer will send out questionnaires randomly, generally to three out of four customers
  - o Request that they contact you once they receive the questionnaire, in which case you will either:
    - Visit them to go through any concerns and help them complete it.
    - Make them a coffee at a convenient time for them to visit the showroom, then discuss and complete the form.
    - Ask them to call you when they are going through the form.
    - Any other way you can think of getting hold of the form. (The reason will become apparent soon)

o   Make a separate follow-up date to ask if the form has been received. It is essential to keep track of the document and if and how it has been completed. Has it been sent yet?

When it comes to accessories that the customer has requested, it is better to present most of them at the point of handover rather than installing them in the car. The exceptions are larger items such as carpet mats or a boot liner; they should be fitted to the car before handover. Otherwise items such as phone cradles or child car seats, should be presented. This gives you the opportunity to demonstrate how they are fitted.

Once all the paperwork is complete you can relax and move on to the best part of the process; demonstrating the controls and essential items to the customer and sending them on their way. A comprehensive handover should diminish the amount of comeback you get from the customer in terms of how things work. However remember, people process information at different rates, so keep it brief. Refer them to their vehicle handbook or offer them the opportunity to revisit certain items if necessary, in the future.

After-Sales Follow Up

Just when you thought it was all over, you will be expected to keep in touch with the customer. It is customary to complete and record a follow up programme, generally in this order:

- 3 days
- 3 weeks
- 3 months
- 12 months
- 18 months
- 2 years
- 30 months
- 3 years

This is designed simply to keep in touch with the customer and continually reinforce your name and dealership. Initially you should be interested in how they are getting on with their purchase and if they have any concerns over the car or associated paperwork. Make sure they are pleased with their purchase and press home the fact that you are there for them if they have any more queries. This will build trust no end.

Start asking if their friends or family are jealous and if they know of anyone who is looking to change their vehicle. It is never too early to ask, especially if you have built up a relationship with them and they take you for the nice cheeky chap that you are. Don't be too embarrassed to ask; it's your earnings and respectability at stake, after all.

All Buyers Are Liars

CSI Questionnaire

The CSI questionnaire has become one of the most important and concentrated-on elements of any modern dealer group, as it is linked to performance bonuses, normally based on quarterly targets. The bonuses available here are linked to vehicle sales achievements and service and parts department profits. The manufacturers not only monitor the customer's response to each dealer, but also they create a league table to show their network how they are performing against their peers.

The demand "from above" for 100% response from the customer, returned to the manufacturer, is ever growing across the nation. At management level the acknowledgement of a failed CSI sends repercussions throughout the company, as it reduces the average result for the group resulting in a possible drop in the league. It's like Manchester United losing to Fulham, as good as that may sound, because it sends shivers down the team's spine to realise they have slipped a place in the premiership.

Generally we are talking about the whole number of dealerships having in excess of 80% CSI returns. Consequently the margin for error is substantially greater if fifteen dealers in your region occupy only twenty percent of the table. A couple of bad results can demote the dealer and group and reduce potential results later on. The emphasis is on knowing what results are being returned, almost predicting what they are going to say. Believe me, some sales people are very good at predicting how their customer will respond, even to the last percentage, which is usually one hundred. How do they manage that? I could tell you, but then I would have to kill you.

Bear in mind that the CSI bonuses normally extend to new cars only. They are monitored for used cars as well, but they do not count towards bonus targets. This is likely to change in the near future though, because manufacturers will realise that with the decline of new car sales, the used car market will become much stronger. It is inevitable that the CSI questionnaire for used car buyers will become more realistic as a tool to measure customer satisfaction. Then all the emphasis will be on that sector, further depleting the sale of new cars.

It has been known for companies to pay a financial reward once a CSI questionnaire has been authorised at 100%. The remuneration differs between dealer groups and the dealerships themselves, but this form of motivation works wonders for any self-respecting sales person. If you are not motivated by the colour of money, then you are in or entering the wrong vocation. You will have the added motivation that if you persistently fail to achieve the required CSI result, then you will be visiting the Job Centre anyway.

Suffice it to say that you are advised to put in the maximum effort with your customers, not only to satisfy management requirements, but also to honour yourself and gain remuneration for your efforts.

Sales Pro Survival Guide

Pre-Judgement

Pre-judgement can be a dangerous habit. Unfortunately we are all guilty of it to some degree or other. Whether we realise we are doing it or not, we often not only make quick judgements in our own mind, but also we voice them to those close by, rapidly harvesting negative feelings about our chosen subject. How many times have you found yourself saying "so and so is a really decent bloke, but I wasn't sure about him at first. I thought he was up his own arse."

Some of you may have used different terminology, but the fact that you pre-judged that person and you were proved to be wrong, demonstrates my point. Cynicism can creep into your tone if you are not careful and it will become apparent, when you meet the customer, that you are not interested in them. This will confirm their opinion of you, as you were also being pre-judged to your detriment, before you met.

Imagine a group of three sales people standing near the entrance of a dealership, chatting among themselves and occasionally looking out of the window. A car slows down and drives onto the forecourt, creeping along at a snail's pace.

"Here we go, look at this goon," John sneers, pointing to the car, which has seen better days.

"What's he doing? Seeing how much everything is before he gets out of his car? It looks like he has been to the moon and back in that thing," Ken joins in.

"Hang on, he is stopping," John confirms.

They all watch briefly before Andy returns to his desk, deciding without saying a word that he doesn't want to get involved. Ken is going on about how he can't believe this arsehole has parked his car right in the middle of the forecourt, among all the cars for sale.

"I know, what a prick! We should get a price board with £99 on it and ask him if he wants us to sell it for him," John sniggers, almost wetting himself laughing at his own joke.

Ken laughs along, adding, "yeah, or tell him the Bargain Car Centre is down the road."

The prospective buyer is wandering round the forecourt now, looking at the choice on show, occasionally looking towards the window, watching the body language of John and Ken. He feels uncomfortable that they are watching him, although he does want to change his car and needs some advice. He continues to walk round and spots a car that he has been considering. He takes a quick look and is impressed enough with the condition to want a look inside.

John advises Ken, who has been distracted by the receptionist, that the knobhead has settled on his old demonstrator. He can't help but inform Ken and Lucy (the receptionist) that this guy has got champagne taste with lemonade money, to which Ken responds by suggesting the guy is a big hitter with a little bat.

As the customer starts walking towards the dealership to ask for the keys, so he can have a better look, he sees Ken pointing and laughing, obviously talking about him with his colleague. With anger building up inside him, making him feel flushed and irritated, he decides to give it a miss and strides back towards his car.

Just before he gets back to the forecourt Andy appears with a notepad, heading towards the car next to his, noting the registration number and price. Standing a few yards away, as the buyer gets back to his car, Andy catches his eye and offers to help.

"I was just going. Didn't think anyone was interested," the buyer proclaims.

"I'm sorry you feel that way, I am certainly interested. Come inside and I will get you a coffee or other refreshment," Andy grovels.

"Ok, coffee sounds good, white with one sugar please," the more relaxed customer agrees.

As a result, Andy sells Brian (the prospective buyer / arsehole / knobhead / big hitter with a little bat) Ken's old demonstrator and earns twice as much as normal for doing so, much to the bemusement of Ken and John.

The other scenario would be for the customer to leave unhappy, as is often the case. I prefer the former scenario as it demonstrates the significance of separating yourself from a group only concerned with negativity. By leaving them to it and keeping an eye on the customer, you will have an opportunity to pounce. He should be more receptive to you because he has bad feelings about the two pointers in the window.

Being of sound mind, Brian naturally prefers to buy off someone who doesn't sneer and laugh at him, while he also gets to prove the point that he can indeed afford to buy this product, despite the condition of his current mode of transport.

He has been pre-judged by John and Ken, maybe even Andy too, but Andy keeps his thoughts to himself and watches a common scenario unfold. John and Ken are left wondering where they went wrong. They did have a good laugh, but now feel like they should have had that deal, because they saw him first. No doubt they would return to their desks to lick their wounds and promise themselves they wouldn't let this happen again.

The good news is that pre-judgement is not necessarily a bad thing, if you don't let it interfere with the way you handle yourself in front of the customer. Just because you have pre-conceived ideas about someone doesn't mean you have to show it. Take up the challenge of seeing if you were right and more often than not you won't be. Relax, take an interest in a potential buyer and see what happens. If you keep your mind open you may be surprised.

As well as sales people pre-judging customers, you also have customers pre-judging sales people. Having experience in this field I can tell you that it is as if you can read their minds. Quite spooky, really. It is possible to read the eyes. A distracted look into space tells its own story, as does a roll of the eyes, or a look down the nose, with head held high. Everyone is guilty of this kind of behaviour.

The main difference is that the customer can pre-judge without any major consequence, because they are the ones spending their cash. This gives them the upper hand of course, but it is a sales person's job to turn their negative misconceptions into a positive and trusting perception of you. Although it's not always that easy, the feeling generated when you first see the nod of agreement to what you are saying or the sight of folded arms opening up and relaxing, is what keeps us going. Without realising it you will sense the changes in body language and automatically increase your efforts in persuasion.

An already disgruntled customer may pre-judge by thinking disparaging thoughts and here are some of the more obvious ones to spot, just by looking at someone's actions and expressions:

- Look at this guy, looks like a right know-it-all:
    o Pouted lips; sideways smirk; slight pause in step

- Oh no, here we go, a sales person:
    o Roll of the eyes; quick change of direction; hand clutching keys

- Leave this to me, love (whispered to partner):
    o Tap of partners arm; moving in front of partner; stern look straight in the eyes

- Better not show any interest:
    o Evasive posture; looking down; using phone as distraction

- Nice one, I can get some information:
    o Looking at you in desperation; half raising an arm then realising they look stupid, you're not a waiter; pointing at a car to attract your attention

As people use risk analysis to determine every action in their lives, it is easy to see why we pre-judge so often. The way we use risk to answer our concerns is twofold. Initially our subconscious mind comes into play; without conscious thought we get a feeling of emotion linked to the act we have just encountered. This feeling is generated very quickly and affects our pattern and train of thought, the extent of which is related to how strong these feelings are. They can leave you with a sharp ache in your gut, hence the term "gut feeling." Your heart will beat faster and may even race; again, this all happens pretty quickly. Once the panic subsides your head will try to interpret and control your thoughts, adding some rationality or logic, or at least trying to. The head is providing conscious thought and usually takes its time to decide your opinion. Indeed it may never truly decide. The gut feeling still remains and often affects your conscious thoughts, whether it is right or wrong. "It's doing my head in" – a classic statement provoked by an indecisive head arguing with the gut.

The brain is pre-programmed this way and has been for thousands of years, so there is no way to negate the thought process of your subconscious; only to diminish the potential harm by considering how your brain operates. It will also be proved right on plenty of occasions, leaving you thinking you are psychic for sensing something with that gut feeling, with your subconscious mind saving you from embarrassment or regret.

It goes back to proving the customer wrong. If you sense you have been wrongly pre-judged, increase your efforts to convert the customer rather than just walking away. If you cannot be bothered, then you will be watching your money walking straight into someone else's pocket, or worse, straight out of the door.

Trust

Trust is a wonderful word, because for some reason it conjures up thoughts of liars and cheats. The mind automatically sees the reverse and goes through its database of negative thoughts about itself and others. Strange, or is that just me?

Trusting colleagues is an important part of a stable working environment. The ability to get on with people in all departments is crucial to success and the quickest way to achieve that, is to build trust. Although it is easier for some people, the secret lies in giving. If you allow people into your thoughts they will feel more emotionally close to you and this will encourage further interaction. Striking up a conversation about things other than work creates an emotion in those who are receiving your interest. This is the personal touch, rather in the same way as the nice feeling you get when someone compliments you, although that feeling may then be superseded by embarrassment.

The will to converse on a more personal level breaks down barriers and builds trust quickly. People who communicate on a personal level are proven to have greater success than those who keep their thoughts and feelings to themselves. I'm not saying you should go around getting personal with everyone (that might get you smacked) but you get the gist. It is about building key relationships in all areas of your business and you can't do that without a certain amount of trust.

Once you have put your trust in a colleague and they appear to trust you in return, you will have much more success when asking for something to be done. Equally you will also feel more obliged to help them in some way or other, so it's scratchy-back time, which is no bad thing. To indulge myself I have two quotes that I heard years back that have held me in good stead:

- "I will trust you until you give me a reason not to."
- "I'd rather be a favour in front, than a favour behind."

Trust is a simple concept in that it will grow if it is nurtured and treated with care, but it will stop dead if it is crossed - as the quote suggests, "until you give me a reason not to." At that point any trusting feelings gained are lost. Like the snake in snakes and ladders, trust will slide right down the scale and will need to be built up all over again.

Watch out for the untrustworthy parading themselves as trusting friends. The snakes are back, but in the grass this time. With more faces than Big Ben they will pretend they can be trusted, by empathising with your plight and then telling anyone who will listen all about your woes, after promising to keep it to themselves. Nice. I'm sure you will spot the snakes in the grass and use them accordingly. For as long as you know of their tendencies, you can use them to get your point across, where necessary, without having to say a word. Keep these people close too, because their gossiping, frenzied approach will feed you key information and as irrelevant as most of it will be, I'm confident some whispers will be precious knowledge to have.

It is important to help others in order to demonstrate your willingness to assist them when you can. Don't be a mug though. There is a fine line between being helpful and being servile. Everyone likes a lap dog to follow them round cleaning up after them. Do not be that dog. It's a degrading thought, so bearing it in mind it should keep you on the straight and narrow. Be your own person, help when you can and request help when you think you're being left to do something on your tod.

We have mentioned trust with the customer earlier so I don't wish to dwell on it too much. Suffice it to say that rules very similar to those regarding your colleagues, apply here in building trust with your customers. The main differences are that the personal touch should be more diplomatic and professional with customers, as you will not have the same kind of relationship with them as you do with some members of your company. (By this I mean platonic relationships…)

So although the personal approach still applies, to avoid unnecessary confrontation it should not be over-played. I suppose that dressing it up as an effective way to build trust, is probably misleading; it is called charm. There, I said it. Some people have it and some people don't. The most effective way of gaining someone's trust is the skilful use of charm. How many people do you know who could "charm the birds out of the trees?" Do you trust them? Chances are, yes, although there may be something not quite right about them. Too good to be true perhaps? You know they could talk you into almost anything. Use these people to help you learn the art of communicating on a personal level, even though the discussion may centre on business.

The other key point is to trust the customer. It is one thing for you to gain their trust, but you also have to be able to trust them. Again, you can use the skills that you use with your colleagues, but as you are starting afresh with each customer you will have to be a lot quicker. You will gain trust with colleagues progressively and slowly, because you have the time to do so. With your customer you need to be swift in interpreting their agenda and as soon as you are providing them with reasons to trust you, you should also be using clever questioning to see if they are trustworthy in their requests.

There is no need to fret if you don't trust them. This will not stop you selling them a car, but it is always a more pleasurable experience if you do trust them. The point is that if you struggle to trust them initially, you may be able to identify why and correct it. Trust is a two-way emotion. The more they trust you, the more relaxed they will be. The more relaxed they are, the less defensive they will be. The less defensive they are, the easier it will be to like them. When you like them, you will start to trust them. And so it goes on. It is a mindset to get to know people; you have to want to do it. If you can't be bothered, then don't bother.

Politics

The joy of politics. And you thought this was a book about the sales process. Well, as in most walks of life politics play a major part of the motor industry, in ways that you could never imagine. However do not despair because I lift the lid on some strange happenings in the wonderful world of a franchised dealership.

The majority of workplace politics are attributed to cliques, in one or another way, shape or form. Inevitably there will be someone who does not fit into the clique or has been excluded by choice. In most cases it is essentially down to a personality clash. The politics come in when one personality decides to affect the other in some way, such as being obstinate or difficult towards them. When people develop an agenda of hatred towards a colleague they can be capable of all sorts of trickery and deceit. I have seen a few nasty moves in the past which you may find entertaining:

- Hiding car documents, to delay the handover for their customer.

- Contacting colleague's customers on colleague's day off, to elicit an easy sale.

- Putting trade plates on a car that a colleague demonstrated, leaving them on overnight, to elicit a warning to them from the boss.

- Taking a telephone call meant for a colleague, and telling the customer it's their day off, in an attempt to hijack the deal.

- Deleting data from a colleague's computer diary so they will forget to follow them up, then guess what?

- Telling the receptionist that a colleague said she was fat.

- Informing the service department that a colleague's customer has cancelled their order, so they had better not do the work requested.

- Insinuating to the boss that a colleague's deal is taking in a real dog of a car in part-exchange, thereby making the boss think he is going to lose money on it.

- Informing a customer that the car they are being shown was brought in from a bereaved child; their dad died in the car.

- Asking for help at every given opportunity but not returning the favour when asked by a certain colleague.

As with most office politics, the adventure into favouritism is enjoyed by the motor trade on a major scale. Nepotism is rare, but not completely absent. There is the usual boys' club in most cases, but here we concentrate on people receiving favoured treatment from the management, in comparison with that of their peers. In political terms, favouritism of subordinates ranks much higher than favouritism between colleagues or between departments, because here rank comes into play and changes the behaviour you would use with a peer. The boss comes in all sorts of guises, but generally the motor trade is renowned for dictatorship style of management. We will explore this in more detail later.

The usual scenario is that the boss will find fault with all the members of his team except for one - their little favourite; the kid who brings the apple in every day. The boss will find it in his heart to display his protégé's every good turn at each and every opportunity. Let's call the blessed one Bobby, just to build a picture.

The gaffer will boastfully tell all that he would have a full team of Bobby's if he could. "All you lazy bastards can get yourselves to the Job Centre and I will just have a team who want to do what I ask."

You will also notice that Bobby doesn't say much and is probably quite embarrassed by his new mate's outpouring of love, but he will keep his thoughts to himself, not wishing to rock the boat. After all, his boss is the captain of this ship and who is Bobby to steer it another way? While he is getting free deals and is allowed to chat the receptionist up as much as he likes, or while the boss is bollocking his colleague for talking to a customer on the phone with his hand in his pocket, he is not going to change anything. The ongoing verbal slaughter of Bobby's work mates is starting to grind people down and the inevitable freezing out of Bobby quickly ensues, courtesy of his sales colleagues. Bobby might be able to do what he likes, but he will be doing it alone from now on.

This scenario may sound childish and you are perfectly correct. It is childish and that is the point. Unfortunately the boss has mentally switched to parent mode and is determined to present his favoured child in the best light while admonishing his other underlings. When he reverts to adult mode he may consider the consequences of his actions, but after a giggle it will be forgotten until next time. The damage is done by singling people out in front of others. It is humiliating, degrading and demoralising. The professional way to do things is to discuss concerns on a one-to-one basis, away from other staff and customers. There is no winner with favouritism. It not only destroys relationships but also it puts at risk the respect that the sales team may have for their manager.

The opposite effect of favouritism, or being out of favour, has an even greater effect on confidence and morale. It is relatively easy to deal with being the favourite, even if you don't want the attention. It is harder to witness someone else being the favourite, but again it is surmountable with the right attitude. However it is extremely difficult to deal with treatment associated with being out of favour. The political agenda of a manager persecuting an employee can last forever, or at least until the goal of outing the unwanted is achieved. Unfortunately it is down to the individual being persecuted to remain resolute in their own abilities, despite the circumstances – or, indeed, to ship out, leave the experience behind and move on.

The outcome depends on the attitude of the individual. Strong characters will talk themselves out of leaving because of the unfairness of it, along with a desire to have the last laugh, hoping that they can become the victor and see off their opponent. The difficulty with this is the hierarchy. The majority of modern businesses are based on backing up the line of command, even if it's known that certain individuals are creating divisions and fostering oppressive behaviour.

Mental deficiency plays a part in how people treat others, or more importantly, how they treat people who they perceive to be more intelligent than they are. If you think you are not as intelligent as someone else there is a tendency to feel threatened. Unconscious resentment can creep into the mindset, altering the behaviour shown towards you. Rise above it and stay polite. You don't have to buy favour with people who resent you, in an effort to change their opinions. This only makes the matter worse, because you will then resent them back for making you tread on eggshells when interacting with their petty little minds. Leave them to their inadequacy and concentrate on developing friendships with those who do not feel threatened by your intelligence.

We can all be capable of jealousy or envy, and unfortunately this is one of the main causes of political behaviour in the workplace. I would be willing to place a bet that you, my reader, at some stage have been the victim of inappropriate behaviour caused by the perpetrator being jealous of your situation, intelligence or skills. It may even come down to the fact that you are better looking than them or that you are capable of getting on with people better than they can. Whatever the reason this jealous streak will appear in many different guises; sometimes it is undetectable, but it will manifest itself in a variety of ways.

More often than not the person harbouring these feelings will treat you with some kind of animosity, trying to put you down or criticise you in front of others. This gives them the feeling of power over you, boosting their ego and making them believe that others will think more of them than they do of you. Unbeknown to them, most people viewing their behaviour will see right through it and realise they envy the person they are constantly castigating. It's a childish game of "I'm better than you and I will demonstrate this to anyone who thinks differently."

The other way people deal with their envy is to suck up to their subject. For whatever reason this person can do no wrong in their eyes and they behave as if they are in the company of a god, agreeing with everything they say and do, to offer their respect and to boost their ego in front of other people. It is not a very good attribute and makes them look like sheep to their peers.

It's one thing being a "yes" person, doing as you're told regardless of your opinion just to keep the peace. People behave in this manner because they don't like confrontation and don't want to be singled out as difficult to manage or high maintenance. It is quite another to pursue the adulation of someone because you secretly want to be them. You will be regarded as a clone by your peers and excluded, due to fear that anything said to you will go straight back to the person you envy, whether it is critical or pleasant.

Greed

Another pet hate of mine is greed. As with most industries based on selling a product or service, it always comes into the equation in many ways and guises. The definition of greed is "extreme desire for something, often more than one's proper share". For me, that defines it perfectly. Early Christian teachings also noted greed as one of the seven deadly sins or capital vices, as they were known. The biblical meaning of greed is applied to the acquisition of wealth in particular.

From an employer's point of view, especially when running the business, greed is mainly attributed to the decisions given to sales people about the deal that is under negotiation. If the salesperson has received commitment from the customer to purchase a vehicle based on a figure discussed between the two parties, then a decision generally has to be agreed by the manager, either in person or via the telephone. This need for agreement has been discussed in the sales process previously. The reason why I bring it up again is that during these conversations there is usually a tendency, by those making the decisions, to get greedy. I can imagine the conversations going on all over the country, something like this:

Sales Manager:	*Are they committed to buying the car today?*
Sales Person:	Yes.
Sales Manager:	*Great, where are you with the deal?*
Sales Person:	They will buy the used car they have driven for £10,500 to change.
Sales Manager:	*What have we offered so far?*
Sales Person:	I presented the figures at £11,000 to change.
Sales Manager:	*Tell them, that's the deal, it's the cheapest car available. I've just reduced the car by £500.*
Sales Person:	OK boss, but I think we could get another £500 for their car and that would make the deal.
Sales Manager:	*Yes, but that is trade profit, why should we give everything away? Just go and deal them, instead of trying to deal me.*
Sales Person:	All I'm saying is that they are not dealing for £11,000, I have tried everything to chip them up and if we don't budge they will walk.
Sales Manager:	*They won't walk, see how you get on, but don't let them go without talking to me.*

This story can only go two ways. Either the customer really wants the car and is genuinely just trying it on, or they throw a paddy and start suggesting you're ripping them off, before leaving with haste. As a sales person this scenario is extremely frustrating, because although you want to sell the car, you don't want your boss to be right in their greedy pursuit of profit. A part of you almost wants the customer to walk because at least you could prove to your boss that he made the wrong judgement and that a bird in the hand is worth two in the bush. (Or was that just me?)

The moral of the story is that it is always a gamble to test a customer's resolve. However much we all like to make money, it should not be with a "take it or leave it" attitude. The profit margin only counts when the deal is done and calculating the potential deal value is futile. All too often managers protect their margins at their cost, by concentrating on how much the deal could make instead of whether the customer's offer makes an acceptable profit. This is the key element that is forgotten when greed takes over. The end result is no profit at all and wasted time for all concerned. As a direct consequence the customer, who felt it necessary to walk, will buy a car elsewhere and pay the amount you were asking, just because they don't want to go back to you. Fantastic! "All that bad feeling because we wanted to make an extra £500!" – a typical, negative response to this experience.

Also consider the side effects of greed. Although in some instances greed is nurtured by customers who feed it, in the majority of cases an attitude of mutual gain would benefit the business. It is easy to say after the fact that the customer was the greedy one and that they wouldn't have dealt anyway. The truth is that a deal could have been struck there and then, albeit with a reduced profit margin. In my mind why take the risk? Why not just get a profitable deal done and reap the benefits of referral business plus the prospect of selling the customer another car in the future. Less really is more. Successful people throughout the world have based their businesses on doing what needs to be done to get the end result. Greedy businesses tend to have a short run of dramatic returns followed by falling into the abyss.

The sales environment is not for the faint hearted. All efforts need to be made to ensure you are not being taken advantage of. Like most careers, the sales environment is full to the brim of arseholes. Ready, willing and able to shaft you, as soon as look at you. Greed is like a plague that nestles inside the brain, almost dormant. It will strike whenever a chance of self-gain appears.

Be prepared for colleagues who will look for opportunities to steal deals from you. This is another way greed can interfere with your success. Some of the people you are working with may decide that the deal you are working on would be better dealt with by them. They will wait until you are off, or with other customers; then they will contact your customer in an effort to offer them an alternative deal. All sorts of excuses and reasoning will come out when you find out, but by then it will be too late, as they would strategically get the manager to side with them. The end result is that you could lose a deal because your so-called friend and colleague decided that nicking your deal is easier than selling a car from scratch. There is absolutely no advantage to that kind of behaviour. In the short term a deal has been done, which is good for the business, but in the long term feelings of ill will spreading through the sales team disrupts productivity.

Then there is the greedy customer. Aren't they all greedy, I hear you ask. The answer is no, they aren't all greedy. There are plenty of decent customers who realise that your company is not a charity and that profit is not a dirty word. The idea of negotiation is for two parties to come to an agreement that suits both sides. Unfortunately there are a select number of customers who will never understand that concept. To them negotiation means taking as much as possible from a deal without offering concessions.

When selling a car there are several ways to negotiate, especially when there is a part-exchange involved. A deal can be attained by reducing the price of your car; offering more money for a part-exchange; including items of value. The problem comes when the customer wants to negotiate on all three, rather than looking at the bottom line.

Let's say that you manage to convince the customer that you are too far apart and you agree a more reasonable figure. Imagine a scenario where the customer has committed to do a deal if you can achieve a specific price to change. You confirm on three occasions that they will buy the car now, if you can get to that price.

Sales Person:	Excellent news; we are in a position to offer you that deal.
Customer:	*OK, great, but you haven't given me any more for my car.*
Sales Person:	We have negotiated on the difference. I have reduced the price to change by £1200 to get to the deal you wanted.
Customer:	*I appreciate that, but I still want £1000 more for my car.*
Sales Person:	We have a finite amount of profit in the car, most of which we have chosen to share with you. I can't offer you any more for your car, because we will move it on for the price we have been offered.
Customer:	*Well, we can't do a deal then.*
Sales Person:	I'm a bit confused.
Customer:	*Why?*
Sales Person:	Well, when we went through the deal you told me three times that if I could get to that figure you would buy the car now. Have I misunderstood your requirements?
Customer:	*No, but the more I think about it the more reluctant I am to give you my car for that price.*

Whatever the outcome, the customer has moved the goal posts. They committed to a deal, then when you confirmed the deal could be done they panicked, thinking it was too easy and that they should have asked for more. Greed, greed, greed. Will you be able to trust this customer the next time they commit?

The chances of a deal are now unlikely and you have the job of telling your manager, who you bullied to get the deal, that you haven't signed them up, despite assurances that they would buy the car now.

Ethics & Morals

This is a great topic for the motor industry. Although the public perception has got better over the last ten years, the car trade is still tainted with the "Arthur Daley" stereotype. Unfortunately in the eyes of the public we are all tarred with the same brush, even after all these years. I suppose it's like market traders being referred to as "Del Boy."

Ethics and morals have not formally been considered when selling cars, or selling anything else for that matter. Whether you are selling cars or coffee or houses, the remit is to get a sale, by hook or by crook.

Morally, not a great deal has changed. The motor industry is still full of sharks that would sell their grannies to make a few pounds. Morals are personal and individual. We all have our own belief systems and we work within those boundaries.

Ethics are a different kettle of fish because international companies have learned to adopt certain ethical codes of practice. These ethics are then passed through all staffing levels to ensure uniformity in attitude and customer service. By doing this the company benefits from a measurable programme designed to provide the best advice at all times. It is also attached to disciplinary procedures to make transgressors accountable.

It is difficult to make people accountable for their moral beliefs but it is perfectly acceptable for a company to set a code of ethics that has to be adhered to by all personnel. These practices are evident among all global manufacturers as they look to build trust with their customers, whom they plan to retain for as long as possible. The difference to the perception of the motor industry has been enormous.

It is not just the manufacturers who have improved their service. Large dealer groups have also written ethical procedures into their staff handbooks and realised that best advice is the only way forward.

The internet has brought with it a much more informed customer, who won't stand for any unethical advice or behaviour. Their choices are greater than previously and they will not hesitate to place their business elsewhere if they feel they have been misled or lied to.

Aside from the ethics and morals of sales people, customers seem to have their own contradictory standards. It is all well and good for potential buyers to dismiss all sales people as liars, but the truth is that they also lie to try to get a better deal. The scruples held by many customers leave a lot to be desired. They will bend the truth, exaggerate or pretend they have been offered better deals elsewhere.

Targets

Targets are a necessary evil when it comes to selling cars, or anything else for that matter. They are a way of challenging a sales team to achieve an overall dealership target, which in turn ensures suitable rewards for all concerned. More importantly they are essential to measure the progress of individuals.

Without targets there is no urgency for anyone to match or exceed the expectations of their employer. They also promote healthy competition within a sales team. Targets are set on a monthly basis and as the saying goes "you're only as good as your last month's sales". Whatever the reasons for not performing and there are always excuses, the figures don't lie.

The motivation for achieving targets will differ among sales people. Some will only consider the financial rewards of achieving their goals, while others will be driven by a desire to be the best seller in the team. Being the number one sales person in a dealership is great for the ego, but ever better for confidence. In my early years of selling cars the coveted number one spot was my be-all and end-all. Over time my motivation became money, due to dramatic increases in my outgoings. (Having said that, it was still very rewarding to be the top dog.)

The other advantage of being number one is that regardless of whether the dealership has performed or not, you will be spared the manager's wrath, which is always a winner.

Do not be under any illusions though; targets are set to be achieved. If they are not attained on consistent basis, the chances are that you will be out of a job. It is not uncommon for dealer groups to promote a three strikes rule. This means that if you fail to achieve your goals for three months in a row, then start looking for an alternative career or try your luck at the dealership next door. It sounds harsh, but that is the motor industry.

Dealer groups use this system not only to incentivise their staff, but also to protect themselves. Employment laws in the UK have changed dramatically over the years, to the benefit of the employee, and as such it is much harder to dismiss staff than it used to be. This is made much easier when the sales person does not achieve an agreed target. The employer will take disciplinary action against the perpetrators each month they fail, until the inevitable final warning is issued. Fail again and look forward to clearing your desk, handing your demo keys back and being dropped off by a colleague.

In my own experience it doesn't matter how much you may have sold, or how much you have done for a company in the past; that's history. There is no loyalty when it comes to under performance. I remember having a particularly bad time consistently for three months, having achieved all expectations for the previous three years. I found myself having a very uncomfortable conversation with a company director and having to reiterate the contribution I had made to the business over the years. Luckily I was given a reprieve and the next month all the hard work I had been putting in finally paid off, placing me back at the top of the pile. Had I not stated my case the business may not have benefited from my efforts. C'est la vie, such is life. Dry your eyes, mate, and move on.

As well as being the big stick to hit you with, the other side effect of targets is how they affect your confidence. The activity and success of all sales people, whether they realise it or not, is your confidence level at any given time. When things are going well and suitable goals have been achieved, the world is great and your confidence will be sky high. This is when a sales person is at their most productive. If they can keep complacency at bay, everything will seem to flow. You will be prepared to say and do things that you wouldn't ordinarily say or do because the prospect of rejection has been diminished in your mind, due to recent results.

The converse can be catastrophic for your confidence, though. A sustained run of bad luck decimates confidence, thereby rendering you almost useless. Sales people are naturally deflated when results do not come their way and even more frustrating is watching your colleagues ripping up trees, making you feel that it must be your fault.

These are the highs and lows, the rollercoaster ride that comes with the territory.

The art is to remain positive because what goes around really does come around and you will get out what you put in. Do not be sucked in by the doom brothers, reinforcing negative feelings. Every dealership has them.

Luck, Luck & More Luck

Luck plays a major part in all of our lives, and it features heavily in the motor trade. Some people believe that you make your own luck. I can't see it myself. Such prophecies are normally suggested by people who have always had their fare share of luck, taking it for granted so much that they don't realise it.

You are either lucky or not, with the qualification being whether you believe it or not. If you choose to believe then you can monitor your luck factor in all areas of your life. It may be that you are particularly lucky with money, or lucky in love. Whichever it is you will probably find that it is countered by misfortune in other areas. A friend's mother once told me "if you are lucky with money, then you aren't lucky in love." Having an ambitious attitude and wanting both, I never agreed, but it has made me wonder ever since.

Do you benefit from circumstances on a regular basis? Or do you have to grind results out?

Are your colleagues sitting back, doing nothing and still getting all the deals? Or are you being starved of phone enquiries, because the receptionist doesn't like you?

I once sought to make myself available during lunchtime, in an effort to get all the phone calls as well as incoming customers. I thought I would make my own luck. After taking sixteen calls, mainly passed through to parts and service, I decided to go for lunch just as my lucky colleague was coming back from his. You know what's coming. He took the next call and dealt the guy, subject to test drive. The customer came and bought the car the following week. It does make me laugh now, but was that my shit luck or his good fortune, or both?

Too much focus on luck, good or bad, distracts people from their end game. It's like having faith; it doesn't do anything for you physically, but it alters your emotional state. If you are feeling particularly lucky, you will suffer from complacency and maybe conceit. If you are challenged by a poor run of luck, you become withdrawn and less confident. Either way you are screwed; so in the words of Don Corleone, "forget about it."

White Flaggers

Due to the wealth of information available now, we have seen a decline in the number of white flaggers who buy cars. This is a specific type of customer who has come to the dealership to buy a car now, without any desire to negotiate or become distracted from what they want to achieve.

The white flagger will have done his homework. They will have a clear idea of the type of car they want, with a maximum budget in mind. The great news is that they will not want to leave until they have purchased a car that suits their needs. Fantastic; as a sales person you cannot ask for more than that. You will know quickly from the initial conversation that the customer is intent on doing a deal today.

Not only will this customer be happy to pay the screen price for the car, but also he will be receptive to any justifiable add-ons. You will be able to convince them to buy a paint protection, warranty and GAP insurance. They may even go for your finance, just to get it all sorted out straight away.

You cannot expect an easier deal than a white flagger, so called because it is like they surrender and wave a white flag upon entering the dealership. Ignore them at your peril. This is another area where luck will prevail.

Whoever happens to be there at the right time, to talk to the customer, will get the deal; it's as simple as that.

Sales Person:	Do you need any help?
Customer:	*Yes, I would like to have a look at a car outside; it's for my daughter.*
Sales Person:	Okay, let's go out and see which one it is.
Customer:	*It's the silver one on the end. Do you think you could have it ready for the weekend? It's her birthday on Sunday.*
Sales Person:	Yes, we could, it has been prepared so we only need to tax it.
Customer:	*Good, then I will take it. What do we need to do?*

Bish, bash, bosh, deal done! It will never get any easier than that and although it sounds a bit too easy, this still happens every now and then. It is soul destroying if you see it happen to a colleague, but elating if you happen to be the respondent. White flaggers are always welcome and when you come across one, it makes your week; but get ready for some loathing banter from the rest of the team.

Management Styles

The diverse network of characters working in the motor industry does provide constant entertainment for the troops. From technicians to valeters to flash gobby salesmen, a car dealership would give TV producers hours of fun for the public to laugh and cringe at. But in true "David Brent" fashion I would prefer to use management styles to show you what sales people are up against.

The Manipulator – "Mr Hal Eluya"

Hal is a rare commodity in this industry due to his ability to do the job on a consistent basis. Always on time, always well groomed, always positive, this guy overwhelms people with his enthusiasm. As a well respected boss with a professional attitude, Hal motivates his colleagues by encouraging their strengths. He dismisses any negativity within the team and promotes action.

In return for such an open minded approach Hal expects hard work and obedience. Make no mistake; he will not be crossed. Any attempts to undermine him will convince him to mess with your head. By using mind games, Hal will control the individuals who don't conform to his way of doing things.

In most cases where the commandant believes a member of staff does not fit into the team, they will be frozen out. This is an old technique that forces someone to leave of their own accord, rather than being fired.

The manipulator can be a pleasant person to answer to, as long as you can do your job and you put in the effort required to succeed. In a difficult arena it is extremely uplifting not to have the additional burden of a nuisance boss.

The sting in the tail is that Hal cannot be trusted. He has more faces than Big Ben. Behind all the charm and benevolence lies a backstabber and a gossip. Anything you tell him will inevitably get twisted into some sort of comical story about you to others. This is one of Hal's favoured methods of getting on so well with people - making them laugh by bitching about their colleagues. It is a useful technique though, I will give him that.

The Bully – "Mr Dick Taitor"

Dick is far more common; in fact you might say "common as muck". Usually angry and obnoxious, he thinks he rules with an iron fist. He has developed this demeanour because at home he is the little man, with no respect from his partner or children. There, Dick gets told what to do and doesn't really feel comfortable in his own home; a bit like a spare part. He's there to provide money and maintain the garden, but not much else. Receiving no love, support or attention frustrates the hell out of Dick, which translates directly into his controlling behaviour at work.

Here, he is the boss and he must be obeyed. Dick sees the workplace as his train set and he is the driver. All efforts are made to reiterate his standing and receive acknowledgement from the subservient.

The bully will encourage people to have their own thoughts only to gain leverage. He constantly criticises and belittles anyone who contradicts his opinions or suggestions. Even if it means he contradicts himself, which Dick does all too often, he seeks pleasure in opposing a remark to gain control of the discussion. He is not altogether unpleasant; it's just that you need to be seen as being a yes person to receive any favour.

Follow Dick at your peril. Due to his contradictory nature he changes the rules as he goes along to match his current state of mind. Unfortunately he suffers from memory loss when reminded that he said something else the day before. If you become his yes man you will also become his bitch, his ally, his trusted spy and a fellow hypocrite.

The Philosopher – "Mr E. Z. Gowing"

Eazy, as he is known, is exactly as it says on the tin. He is calm, collected and always willing to express himself through self-assured rhetoric. He manages with a tolerant, almost patronising manner, but generally lets the business roll on without interference. Mr Gowing tends to bore his staff with endless renditions of the same ancient proverbs, which do nothing to motivate anyone but himself.

The philosopher doesn't expect a lot. His laid back approach allows sales people to complete their own deals, which isn't a bad thing. As long as he can show a profit, or release a problem car, he is as happy as Larry. You won't have to suffer any personal attacks from Eazy; he is far too intellectual to partake in that kind of behaviour.

Spending your time with Eazy is like sitting butt-naked on ice; it is tantalising but numbing. A wander into his eccentric world can be exciting but nothing actually gets done. He procrastinates tirelessly, then wonders where the time has gone.

All concerns brought up within the team will be tactfully put off. Raised voices are hushed with a soothing calmness, but the issue is left unresolved. By sitting on the fence, Eazy is absolved from any confrontations. Anger does build up within him, but he tends to go quiet until the drama subsides. If he has to make a judgement, it will usually be very diplomatic.

The Ego – "Mr Lou Catmy"

"Open both doors; he is on his way in". Bighead is back and he looks like he is on a mission. Let me introduce you to the busiest man in Britain, Lou Catmy. Although he is always well presented, he does think he is thinner than he actually is and as such suffers from tight suit syndrome. If he has to stand and listen to a female colleague for any length of time, he will be sucking his stomach in and posturing like a peacock.

Lou is the smuggest prick on the planet. He is not that bad at the job of managing people, because he does it in a pleasant manner. He contributes to the success of the team and is always happy to talk to the customers. Mr Catmy wants to be liked and on the face of it he is quite likeable, in the sense that he is funny to laugh at.

In a crowd Lou will become acutely jealous if he is not the centre of attention and will insult those who are with petty jibes here and there, in front of an audience, in an effort to win support. He has delusions of grandeur and considers himself quite the Lothario. What he doesn't realise is that women find him sexist, cheesy and repulsive. His groomed hair that attempts to disguise his bald patch, his leathery lizard skin and his overpowering aftershave do nothing to endear the ladies.

The way to keep Lou on your side is to massage his ego now and then. I don't mean arse lick him as often as possible. I mean a comment here and there. If you need something, always mention how busy he is and how you are sorry to interrupt him. Keep your distance and keep under his radar. If you want to get his goat, then embarrass him in front of someone. The ego gets upset when his integrity or pride are challenged; that's when you will see him erupt into a public show of contempt.

The Incompetent – "Mr Ivor Complecks"

Ivor is one of those characters you just can't win with. He is so down on his luck that you feel like ending it for him. It is hard to converse with someone as pessimistic and self-loathing as Ivor. How he has achieved his level of seniority is a puzzle. His work ethic is to hide away completing and analysing reports all day, with the minimum of fuss. He is looking forward to returning home as soon as he can to finish that bottle of vodka off, which he started last night.

Due to his irritable behaviour, his expectations are varied and constantly changing. He could demand something urgently, and then question its relevance when it has been supplied. Forgetful, moody, sloppy and tired, this busy fool can't focus on anything for a sustained period. He alienates employees with his endless negativity. The end of the world is nigh.

Outside work his troubles continue. He is lonely and bitter, without friends; he is a regular Billy Nomates. This is why he has such a pessimistic outlook on life. No one has done him any favours. He has got to where he is by working hard and impressing the right people. He will be damned if he is going to let someone take all that hard work away.

He is yet another type of manager to avoid as much as you can, albeit for different reasons. If there is any luck in the world, sense will prevail and the company will move this confidence zapper on. He is out of his depth and in need of a new career. The motor industry relies on the confidence of its sales people to succeed and negative forces at management level must be eradicated.

The Bare-Faced Liar – "Mr Bill Shutter"

Every dealership has its liars, or fibbers, for want of a better expression. If they are colleagues then you can take them or leave them; if they are your boss then that's more difficult to deal with. Bill is a lively character. He is charming, debonair and occasionally very funny. People do warm to him, at least initially.

Bill has a degree in one-upmanship. If you have a sheep, then he has a farmyard. If you have a Michelin star, then he has two Pirelli stars. His dad is harder than your dad. His Achilles heel is a wanton desire to prove he is considerably better than you. To do this Bill meanders through a "Walter Mitty" existence, making stories up as he goes along. He invents scenarios from the past to reinforce his tremendous skills.

The bare faced liar is incapable of disguising his expressions when recounting a heroic mission. You can see his eyes rolling around his head. You can almost hear his brain churning, thinking of the next exaggeration. As an ex-serviceman Bill never tires of reminding his sales team of the time when he raced up Mount Snowden so fast that when he got to the top he was sent back down to help his friends. When he returned down the mountain he found his best mate exhausted. To make sure his friend did not get into trouble, Bill threw him over his back and carried him up to the top. He even managed to get back up there before anyone else had finished. "Wow, that is awesome Bill!" He set the RAF record for a mile, of 4 minutes 30 seconds, up a mountain, with full kit and backpack.

Best advice? Just nod, smile and make him feel better about himself. Or let your body language send him the message, that you would rather cut your eyelids off and face the sun, than listen to any more of his bullshit.

The Promoted Friend – "Mr Pat Ronising"

Pat is a colleague who has been working as a sales person for a couple of years. His persistent efforts in arse licking senior management and directors have secured him a promotion. Now that he has taken responsibility for the department, you notice that he has changed his approach towards his so-called friends from the sales team. He hopes to distance himself from those he may need to admonish.

Pat expects his staff to carry out his wishes, despite their irrelevance, the instant he requests them. It doesn't matter how important your current workload is, there will be constant reminders to do as you are told or face the consequences. His controlling approach towards his former colleagues does not endear him to them, but he is not here to win friends. In Pat's mind, he has a job to do and he will stop at nothing to prove to his superiors that he has the skills required to do that job.

The friend becomes the foe.

His days no longer consist of laughing at customers and helping out on the pitch. We have moved on to elaborate, conceited speeches every morning, noon and early evening; a disgusting self indulgence that oozes from every pore. The smug look on Pat's face grows every time he sits in his "Sir Alan" chair, inside in the warmth. A stand-up sales person should give him the opportunity to shine and applaud success, but somehow even Pat isn't confident that success will prevail.

The Relic – "Mr Dino Sore"

Dino is an aggressive sales manager living in the past. Everything he says and does is based around old techniques and clichés. He was trained in the early eighties using the Pendle system, which was a highly pressurised form of selling. Customers are ruthlessly bullied into purchasing on the day, by any means necessary.

The sales team are expected to close customers at the first attempt and any failure to do so results in extensive questioning. Dino insists on breaking down the sale to infuse his closing tactics. An example would be placing change in front of the customer to demonstrate the daily difference being discussed. "We are only talking about 58p a day. That's how close you are from owning this car."

Despite not moving with the times, Dino does have the ability to manage the team. He takes responsibility and helps out with the day to day forecourt maintenance, leading by example. Unfortunately his help soon becomes interference by always having to be right. You will need to be focused and prepared to succeed under such an aggressive old school boss, as he has no intention of moving into the twenty first century.

On a personal level he dresses like he has been frozen in time since the eighties. All Farah trousers and brogue shoes, Gabicci polo shirts and Ray Ban Wayfarers. In his late thirties, he struggles to attract females younger than him and ends up going from one short relationship to another, usually with divorcees over five years his senior.

All Buyers Are Liars

Why Ask?

As an afterthought, I have always wondered if people realise what their requests entail. Have you ever been asked to do something which takes a considerable amount of time to perfect? Then when you have completed the task and are pleased with your results, the person who asked dismisses your work without even looking at it.

Why ask?

There is nothing more frustrating than a customer asking you to put together a deal for them, only to find in the end that they had no intention of purchasing a car for whatever reason. Some people find it difficult to be honest about their budget, so as a defence mechanism they play along, suggesting the figures being discussed are within their range. They will let you commit them to doing a deal on the day, then back out at the last minute, when you confirm the bottom line figure and ask for their credit card.

- *"Oh well, we will have to go home and talk about it."*

- "So let me just get this straight. You were happy to drive our car. You were happy for me to appraise your car. You confirmed that you were both in a position to buy the car now, subject to figures. You were happy to discuss how you intend to pay for the car. You told me you have your credit card with you and a deposit is no problem. You let me ring around to get the best price for your car. You were happy for me to negotiate a discount for you from my manager. You had plenty of time to discuss your funding methods with my business manager. Yet now you suddenly want to go away and think about it."

Why ask?

You're probably thinking I am being tough. People have the right to consider their purchase before signing up and leaving a deposit. You are absolutely right and that is more than reasonable considering cars are such an expensive item. The problem with that argument in this case is that the chances of seeing the customer again are slim or none. And slim just left town. Due to an inability to be honest in the first place, this customer wasted everyone's time, including their own. Any attempts to follow them up by phone will be ignored. Even the sneakier sales person, who dials them without caller ID, will be given a feeble excuse for not buying the car.

Unfortunately this type of behaviour is on the increase due to the availability of information. Customers are led to believe that if they shop around they will get better deals. My criticism of this way of doing business is that there is no allegiance to the people who make the most effort to get your business.

As a sales person I prefer to give my business to the person who has given me the best advice and taken my enquiry seriously. Even if I am able to buy the item cheaper elsewhere, I will pay a premium to buy it from the person who looked after me in the first place.

The other annoying habit in this category is the person who asks for your advice, then argues with you when you give them your opinion.

Why ask?

Customer:	*I'm after a bit of advice.*
Sales person:	Ok, fire away.
Customer:	*What miles per gallon will this car do?*
Sales person:	You should average about 30 mpg around town.
Customer:	*I bet you don't, not with that engine. I don't reckon you will get more than 25.*
Sales person:	Why ask then, if you already know?

It would be great to be able to say that without offending the customer, but sadly you will need to be more diplomatic.

Lie Detection Masterclass

The main danger of a misleading customer is three-fold:

1. They can trap you into doing all the work for nothing – wasting your time and energy.

2. They can take your attention away from genuine customers – costing you real sales opportunities.

3. They can force you to give up all potential profit under false pretences.

So, if you want to save yourself from spending time and effort on a prospect who simply isn't interested in buying then it comes down to basic qualification or disqualification.

Trust your instincts and press them harder if you think they are giving all the right signals but with no intention to purchase.

Slow them down a bit and take control. You should be able to recognise the giveaway signs that betray them.

They may be talking a good job, but does their body language mirror what they are saying? The eyes are the window to the soul, so watch them carefully.

5 General B.S. Indicators

1. Tell Tale Phrases

If I say to you now, "Do not think of a pink Mercedes." What's the first image that springs to mind? Exactly – this is known as negation and NLP has shown that humans simply "can't do a don't" So, when you hear somebody saying things such as, "To tell you the truth", "To be perfectly honest" and "Why would I lie to you?" you can be pretty certain what's on their mind.

2. Misdirection

Taking negation one step further – a liar may open a statement starting with, "I don't want you to think that…" but often that's exactly what he wants you to think! So, whenever someone makes a point of telling you what they're *not* doing, you can be pretty sure they're doing exactly that!

3. Relaxation

The liar becomes more relaxed as soon as the subject is changed. People who are hiding something will be happy to change the subject whereas those who are being honest generally welcome further discussion.

4. Duplication

Watch out for duplication of numbers when a person tells you facts. You'll often find that the numbers are the same or multiples of one another. Watch out when facts relating to time, day and price have unusual similarities.

5. Anxiety

If a customer is anxious then his breathing may appear unnatural, swallowing becomes difficult, he may clear his throat unnecessarily and his ability to focus and pay attention can be diminished. Of course, some people have heard such bad things about car salesmen that they could genuinely be nervous! But if their behaviour changes only once they've said something that could be misleading then a lie is possible.

7 Non-Verbal Clues That Suggest Deception

Non-verbal behaviour varies widely from person to person so just because you see *one* thing from this list it doesn't mean you're dealing with a liar.

In fact, in isolation, many of the following 'clues' may be harmless, habitual actions that carry no specific meaning at all. So, just remember that just because someone avoids eye-contact it doesn't necessarily mean they're lying: they could just be shy or *you* could be making them feel uncomfortable!

However, if your customer displays several (and especially all) of the following clues then chances are they're not telling you the whole truth.

1. Eye Spy

A customer who is lying may do everything possible to avoid making eye contact. Alternatively he may make too much eye contact in an effort to overcompensate for this well known 'tell' in order to convince you of his honesty.

2. Caught Red Handed

A liar's hands may go up to his face or mouth – unconsciously trying to 'cover up' things that could give him away. He is also unlikely to touch the chest with an open hand and if trying to appear casual may shrug a little (or a lot) as he talks. Touching the nose or scratching behind the ear are things we've all heard about – but the customer may simply have an itch!

3. The Wrong Time At The Wrong Place

You've all seen a wooden actor delivering his lines and getting the timing wrong – well unless your customer is a trained and accomplished actor their delivery is likely to be wooden too. So spot for a delay between the 'line' and the 'action'. The timing between a liar's gestures and words may be out of sync. If the appropriate facial expression comes after the verbal statement then it provides a further clue that a fib is being told.

4. Pinocchio Would Be Proud

Moving in a mechanical fashion indicates a conscious, rehearsed or deliberate movement rather than a natural unconscious one. So, if your customer seems to be acting and moving a bit like a puppet then be on your guard.

5. Written All Over Your Face

A liar's facial expression may not always match his words. Frowning when saying "I love it!" is a good indicator that there's a mis-match between the words and the emotion. When lying expressions will also be limited to his mouth area, rather than the whole face when he is feigning certain emotions such as happiness, surprise and interest etc.

6. Acting Shifty

A liar may be reluctant to face you and may instinctively turn the head or shift the body away. If a lie has been committed the accused will probably slouch; he is unlikely to stand tall with his arms outstretched while committing a lie. The customer may also be moving away from you – possibly in the direction of the nearest exit.

7. Pointing To Honesty

While seemingly rude – pointing can often provide a clue to your prospects honesty. A liar will rarely point a finger at the person that he is trying to convince. So if the customer starts pointing at you – this could be a good sign that he really *is* unimpressed with the PX valuation you just gave for his car.

4 Conversational Lie Detection Strategies

As I've already said, clues alone are no reason for you to mistrust a prospect. So, if you feel like doing more detective work before cutting your sales presentation short (and saving yourself from wasted effort) then you may like to try these on for size.

1. Ask For Specifics

Ask your customer clear and specific questions related to his statement. If he is lying, he'll take a while longer than seems natural to answer because he first has to recall his response mentally to be sure it matches.

So, if you think a customer is making up a 'better offer' from another dealer simply ask, "Who?" Once he answers any specific question such as this, ask for more detail. If he's lying, he'll take his time answering (making up) a response. He'll also try to keep to generalities (not giving names, dates, times etc) because made-up stories don't have details; they never happened!

2. Offer A Lie As Bait

Make up a fact, that sounds perfectly reasonable and ask the customer to comment on it. For example, if you wanted to know if someone really did get a better deal at XYZ Dealers down the road then you could mention that you really like the un-missable 'Red '89 Mercedes 300SL R107' they've recently put on show there. As soon as he validates your claim in an attempt to back up his story, you know that he's lying. Otherwise he would simply say that he doesn't know what red Mercedes you're talking about.

3. Believe Then Ask For Proof

Another option is to take what the customer says as fact and request proof, but in a very non-threatening manner. For example, in the case of the person who claimed he had got a better deal from XYZ Dealers, you might let him know that you would love to see their quotation to see how they managed such a low price or in order to see if there's any way you can match or beat them. If he offers up a reason why you can't see the quotation there almost certainly isn't one.

4. Feed The Lie

Elaborate on a 'fact' that a customer has already offered by providing some additional information that wasn't offered or is possibly untrue. For instance, you could say, "So XYZ offered you £3,500 for your old car?" When previously he said they offered £3,000. If he just goes on without correcting you, then you know that he may be lying or, at the least, is willing to lie to get a favourable deal now.

Buyer's Guide

Homework

As a customer there are several ways to approach a dealer when you are considering your next purchase. It is advisable to plan ahead to ensure you get the best out of the experience, as well as getting a deal that you are happy with.

It is wise to do your homework beforehand. You will need to know the following:

What Type Of Car You Are Interested In?

- ☐ 3 door
- ☐ 5 door
- ☐ Saloon
- ☐ Estate
- ☐ Coupe
- ☐ Convertible
- ☐ 4x4
- ☐ MPV
- ☐ Pick-up
- ☐ Van
- ☐ You get the idea

What Age Of Car Do You Want?

- ☐ New
- ☐ Used, under a year old
- ☐ Newest car for your budget

Which Type Of Engine Do You Prefer?

- ☐ Petrol
- ☐ Diesel
- ☐ Alternative (Electric, Hydrogen etc.).
- ☐ Flexible

Which Transmission Do You Prefer?

- ☐ Manual
- ☐ Automatic
- ☐ Flexible

How Much You Want To Spend?

- ☐ Ideal budget
- ☐ Maximum budget

How You Intend To Pay?

- ☐ Cash, via bank account
- ☐ Hire purchase
- ☐ PCP (Personal Contract Plan)
- ☐ Personal loan from your bank
- ☐ Loan from family

What Do You Want To Do With Your Car?

- ☐ Part-exchange with the dealer
- ☐ Sell it privately
- ☐ Sell or give it away to family / friend
- ☐ Keep it
- ☐ Scrap it

How Much Do You Expect To Get For Your Car?

- ☐ Research trade valuations
  (www.wewillbuyyourcar.com)
- ☐ Research private sales (local newspaper)
- ☐ Research retail prices (manufacturers' websites)

When Do You Want To Purchase?

- ☐ Immediately
- ☐ Within The Next Month
- ☐ More Than A Month

Who Else Should Be Consulted?

- ☐ Wife
- ☐ Partner
- ☐ Accountant
- ☐ Business partner
- ☐ Children

What Options Must The Car Have?

- ☐ Satellite navigation
- ☐ Window airbags
- ☐ Hands free phone facility
- ☐ Parking sensors
- ☐ Integrated child booster seats

Colour Preferences?

- ☐ Likes
- ☐ Dislikes

Know What You Want

It is sensible to consider all your preferences before you make your initial enquiry. All of the aforementioned items will come up during your search so you will save time considering them beforehand. I have mentioned the timing element of your purchase because there is no point making an enquiry until you know when you wish to change. If you know that you are not in a position to purchase for at least six months, maybe even a year, then any information you gain at this early stage is irrelevant, as it will change dramatically when you actually come to buying.

If you intend to purchase a new car and you have specific needs, you may need to place a factory order. Prestige manufacturers may not be able to supply exactly what you want, so find out how long it may take to get a car built to order. This information will be available online from the manufacturers. If you are more flexible and don't want to wait for a car, there will be a wider choice available. In this case you will need to identify which options are necessities and which are only preferences. There is no point in considering a car and then finding out at the last minute that a vital requirement is missing.

Doing your homework is recommended to save you time when you make your initial enquiry. With so many details of the purchase to consider, the more information you have, the easier the transaction will be. The salesperson will also take you more seriously when they realise you know exactly what you want and exactly how you intend to pay for it. When dealing with sales people it is important not to show any vulnerability or indecision, because they will see it as a weakness and take advantage of your doubts. They are trained to take control of the sale and will qualify your needs. This stage becomes so much easier for both parties when you are clear about the type of car, maybe even the exact model and what you are looking to achieve with the deal.

There are several ways to gain the information required. If you are computer literate the easiest way is to search the internet, which will give you all the data you will ever need. You may want to visualise your next car, if your needs are not that specific. It may just be a case of not knowing what you fancy until you see it. Go round a few dealerships to see what you like, but make sure you make it clear you are just looking around. Take the literature you need to get additional details about the cars you like. It is advisable not to give any personal details until you are more informed. Take a business card by all means, but leave it at that.

Look through the data you receive and eliminate any cars, engines, colours, options or body styles that you find unsuitable. Initially your selection process should be more about what you don't want, until your choices are defined at which point you can then decide which car you prefer and which presents the best value.

Another major consideration about being prepared is that you will be well informed when you start the buying process. You will be able to make better judgements about the information you receive from sales people and dealerships in general. Dealers will promote the cars they want to move on and if that car suits you there should be a good deal to be had, but if it doesn't meet your criteria then dismiss it early.

Initial Enquiry

The initial enquiry should be made by phone. By calling a dealership ahead of your visit you will be able to set the tone for your purchase early on and establish early rapport with the sales person. The aim of this conversation is to book an appointment to discuss your requirements in person at a suitable time for both parties. Rather than visiting unannounced, this will ensure you don't have to wait around if they are busy or risk being ignored if the sales team can't be bothered. By booking time with a sales person they will get prepared for your visit, which will make the experience more enjoyable.

Try not to offer too much information straight away. Introduce yourself by all means and make a note of the sales person's name. You will get an impression of the person you are dealing with and how they perform on this call. The new breed of professional sales people, developed by dealer group and manufacturers' rigorous training, should be using well rehearsed techniques to get essential information from telephone sales enquiries. If a sales person does not ask you for your name, address, phone number and e-mail address, at this initial stage, then do you trust them to look after your interests when you visit? Probably not. If they cannot be bothered to do the job properly now, you can assume they will not be prepared when you see them face to face.

Where possible, try to set an appointment that will allow the best use of your time. Mid morning or mid afternoon are usually safe bets. Dealers have a sales team meeting every morning, which is designed to keep records of recent activity and plan for the day ahead. It is also an opportunity for the team to be informed of new offers and incentives being introduced by the company or the manufacturer. For that reason you should avoid early morning appointments. Lunchtime is also a time to avoid due to the distraction of a hungry stomach. Minimise these distractions by visiting after you and the sales person have eaten.

And never visit late in the day, if it is avoidable. This presents the biggest distraction of all, because the sales person will be wondering how long this is going to take and will be cutting corners to make sure he can get away on time. More often than not the sales team are always responsible for securing the building and locking up, which may involve moving a few cars, checking that windows and doors are locked, alarming the building, securing the building and pulling up entrance posts or closing a barrier. These procedures take time and will inevitably be playing on the sales person's mind, making them edgy and flustered.

Getting the best out of the buying experience relies on constant, uninterrupted focus from both parties. Only then will you feel satisfied that you received the best customer service. So, opt for an appointment at 10am or 2pm.

Once you have confirmed the appointment time you must make sure the sales person will have a suitable car available for demonstration. If you have a particular car in mind ask them to ensure it will be there and ready to test drive. Consider your language when asking about car availability. "Can you ensure that a car is available, because we may want a test drive?" This will tell the sales person that you are not guaranteed to buy the car on this visit. You have indicated that you may want to drive the car, but then again you may not. You don't want them to think you are a white flagger, do you? You want to be seen as a challenge to ensure the best efforts are made to get your business. This is the second biggest expenditure next to a house, so make sure the sales person earns their money, by convincing you the car is right and the deal is justified. It will be a wasted visit if the car is not available when you get there, so plan ahead to avoid disappointment. If you have made an appointment in a week or so, call again to re-confirm it with the sales person, as they may have forgotten all about you. Give them a gentle reminder just in case.

It is all in the planning, so when you arrive at your appointment, you will be eager and excited and so will the sales person. They will have informed the team and their manager that they have an appointment and will feel confident about selling you a car. Everyone is motivated and ready for action. Come on, let's have it. Even I am getting excited.

Appropriate Behaviour

My intention is not to teach grandmothers to suck eggs. I don't like eggs, well I don't mind the yolk, but that's a different story. By appropriate behaviour I mean it is advisable to remain open, calm and understanding when you're on the verge of parting with this amount of money.

When you arrive at your appointed time you should be greeted promptly by the sales person. Let's say you are meeting James Frederickson today, but we shall call him Jim. He will introduce himself and get you seated at his desk, or in a quiet meeting area. You will be offered refreshment. Although you may prefer to see the car straight away, it is best to play along and enter into a discussion with Jim. He won't have a script but he will be keen to ask open questions and find out more about you and what you are interested in. This is your opportunity to find out more about Jim. You should get him on your side to get the best results later when he negotiates with his boss. His intention is to make you feel obligated to buy from him, so it is sensible to make him feel obligated to help you get concessions.

Hopefully Jim will take you along the sales process properly. Have a look at the first chapter of the book, if you haven't already, for the finer details of the steps he is likely to take. To recap briefly, Jim will take all your details and start making notes on a company appraisal form. He will want to know if you are part-exchanging your car and if you are, you should be prepared with the details he needs. Where possible try to give him the most accurate information; this will prevent any loss of money for your car when you trade it in. Although the dealer will check most of the registration data for your car, there may be elements they cannot check on the day. Once they realise you have misinformed them, detrimentally, they will ask you to pay for any subsequent losses.

There is no benefit gained from lying or exaggerating about your car. Jim will be going round it with a fine toothed comb, checking tyre tread levels, paintwork, windows, mirrors, electrical items, tools, service history, MOT, registration document, road fund licence, engine compartment and interior condition. Part-exchange appraisals are taken very seriously by dealership managers and any sales people found guilty of wrongly identifying a vehicle can be disciplined or fined. The sales manager has overall responsibility, but he will blame Jim.

Be aware that Jim may also spot poorly repaired bodywork. If your car has had accident damage it should not present a problem, as long as it has been repaired properly at an authorised bodyshop. The moral issue of whether you advise the sales person of this fact depends on your own standpoint. The normal procedure is to be honest about any damage pointed out to you by the sales person, if you are aware of it. Accidents happen, but poor repairs will need to be rectified further down the line, so the market value of the car will drop accordingly.

It is not the best time to start alarm bells ringing when your vehicle is being appraised. If you have had authorised repairs then why mention it? There are millions of cars available for sale that also have had accident damage. If you can't spot the repairs then you don't worry about it and neither will they.

Jim will also need to drive the car, just to make sure it feels right. It is good practice for them to ask you to go with them. He will want to build rapport with you and probe you for more information. You might find his conversation pleasant, then again you may not, but there is nothing wrong with a bit of idle chat. You get the opportunity to find out a bit more about Jim, too. People buy from people they like and if you get on well, the negotiation process will be more relaxed and open.

Remain aloof if you are asked any pre-closing questions. Jim may slip in a statement designed to gauge where you are in the buying process, such as "we could have the car ready for the weekend if you like." Nice and smooth. Your response should be guarded but optimistic. You want Jim to believe there may be a deal here and now, but don't give him too much confirmation. If he feels that you are not going to buy today, he will give up and go through the motions. If he thinks that you are definitely dealing today he will relax by taking an assumptive approach, which generally means less compromise when negotiating.

You could respond by saying "we would like it for the weekend but the decision will be based on how well you do with the deal." This reinforces that you are prepared to purchase, but only on your terms. More to the point you are also telling Jim that he is responsible for convincing you. Let's have some obligation. You have basically agreed pre-contract terms. You intend to purchase the vehicle if he negotiates with his manager.

The great thing is you can walk away at any point, because you determine whether his deal is to your satisfaction or not. Win-win.

Finally, you will get the chance to pore all over the car that you have been thinking about for a while now. It's touchy-feely time. Jim will walk you round the car first and with any luck he should point out some of the things that are important to you. I say with any luck, because he should have been listening to your preferences during your discussions. Take this opportunity to see if there is anything missing from the car, in terms of additional items that you definitely want. Make sure they are fitted to this car and that they work. Also look for the items you thought were just a preference. Note any smaller items the car doesn't have that you would like. You may be able to use them as a negotiating tool later on.

The test drive will make or break the purchase. Hopefully the car will surpass your expectations. Make sure all electrical items work and ask Jim to demonstrate the options you are not familiar with, especially if it is fitted with satellite navigation. Test him on that one. This may present a comedy moment if he is not conversant with the system.

The best negotiators say the least. Keep your cards close to your chest. Try to avoid forming opinions until you have all of the information, at which point you can digest it. Use the figures you put together before your visit to compare with what has been presented to you. You will know straight away whether you are close or light years away. Don't say anything.

Getting The Best Deal

When it comes to negotiation a lot of people miss the point completely. The explanation of negotiation is "a mutual discussion and arrangement of the terms of a contract or agreement." The idea is that two parties have a discussion until both agree terms. This implies that even if one party stands firm and the other agrees to their conditions that would still count as negotiation.

Personally, I don't buy into that theory. If you look back further in time, people refer to the art of negotiation as mediation between two extremes, or a discussion of possibilities, which means both sides will use concessions in order to reach a mutual understanding. If one side has put their terms forward, then stated they are not prepared to deviate from those terms, but the other party agrees, then that does not constitute a negotiation. The accepting party has merely agreed to the deal because their need for the item being discussed is so great that they are prepared to buy it for the asking price. This is the exact scenario that we see along the high street on a daily basis. A standard tin of baked beans costing 10p will be 10p or nothing. You either want them or you don't. If you asked the shopkeeper if he could do it for 7p he would run you out of his shop.

The true definition of negotiation is when two parties discuss the reasons for their terms, then find a suitable compromise that makes them both happy. What may be important to you is not necessarily important to the sales person. I will use an orange as an example. Two people are negotiating over an orange. Both parties feel that they need the whole orange to fulfil their requirements. They have reached a stalemate until one asks the other what they need the orange for. The other person says he needs the juice to make a drink. Eureka. While he needs the juice the other person only wants the skin to use as zest. They share the orange but end up with exactly what they originally hoped for.

When you sit down to discuss the deal with Jim you should take time to digest the information he has given you. Do not rush in with rash opinions before you know the full package. There will be several elements to the deal that can be used as leverage. By keeping quiet and contemplating your response, Jim will be starting to feel uneasy. He will attempt to close you by saying "can we have your business?" Assuming you have decided this is the car you want to buy, then your answer should be "yes, but not on those terms." Jim will naturally ask what terms you were hoping for.

At this stage it is prudent to remove any items you have been offered that you hadn't included in your own calculations. Even if you like the products, take them out of the equation and consider them later, when you have agreed the deal. If you refer back to my section on negotiation I have illustrated a deal proposal that is universal in the trade these days. This will show you the items that are sold separately. The dealer's intention is to get you to purchase as much as they can, to increase their profit and achieve certain targets. You should be concentrating on the specific items you have allowed for while preparing your figures.

Now you have removed the unnecessary products, recalculate the bottom line. By this I mean the price to change. When part-exchanging your car you will be offered a trade price, which will be lower than you had imagined. You will also know the screen price for the car you are buying, which will probably be too high. Rather than trying to negotiate on each item, you should base your arguments on the final cost.

It is difficult to advise the amount of discount to ask for because there are so many variables. The dealer only has a certain amount of profit in the cars they are selling, which on new cars could be anything from 5% to 15%. Calculating the profit they will have on a used car is nearly impossible as it will depend on its value when they purchased it, how long they have had it, preparation costs and their desire to sell the car. If it is a desirable and rare model, they will want to maximise the profit, but if it an outdated convertible in the winter, then they may be prepared to make a loss. There is no point getting hung up on how much the dealer is going to make, because for the purposes of your purchase it is wholly irrelevant.

Check through the notes you made prior to visiting. You can request some time to consider the figures; just ask Jim. He will not be offended; in fact he will be pleased that you haven't walked out yet. You should have two figures in your mind. Firstly your ideal price to change and secondly your maximum budget. Compare your figures with his and make an offer that you feel you are comfortable with.

If that sounds like a cop out, it isn't. As I explained it is not for me to suggest what you can get away with, as it is just as likely for me to under deliver as it is to exceed your expectations. If you want the car and it is within your reach, then buy it and start enjoying it as soon as you can. If you can't negotiate within your budget, then you could always see what the monthly payments will amount to. If that fails, then look at an alternative. Jim will be only too pleased to find you something else, rather than losing you altogether.

Keeping Your Promises

To make the relationship with the sales person and the dealership a pleasant one, you should be prepared to keep your promises. If you intend to stay with the manufacturer you have chosen, it is always a good idea to build strong links with the dealer. This will improve the service you receive when you need a service, loan car, recovery, parts and accessories. It is like anything else. The treatment you receive is directly related to how you get on with the staff.

Customer service is regulated in the extreme, by the company and by the manufacturer. Performance is monitored for sales and service in the form of a seemingly endless questionnaire. The intention is to see if you were completely satisfied with your experience. If you were, then say so, there is no point beating around the bush. The results of these forms relate to the person that you dealt with and they may be entitled to rewards if they achieve a certain percentage.

It all seems very American to me - the idea that you should be "completely satisfied"… a bit "have a nice day-ish." So as a Brit I would be tempted to write down satisfied instead, because we are never completely satisfied, are we?

Yes, we are!

If you say, "I'm happy with that, thank you very much." Then you are, blatantly, completely satisfied. That's why it is on the form. It's frustrating to think that the person who looked after you may not receive a bonus because the customer didn't think it was right to give them top marks.

Keeping your promises also relates to the deal itself. If you have committed to a deal and then feel bad about it, don't just cancel the order in a moment of madness. Consider why you purchased it in the first place. Also think about how you would feel if someone said they would buy something from you, and then you never heard from them again. If however, your wife realises what you've done and bans clacker for a month, then do the decent thing and discuss the possibilities with the sales person. They will learn a valuable lesson about qualifying you better, early on. Did they ask you if there was anyone else to consider?

My final point is to suggest keeping your options open with regard to your part-exchange. Once you have signed the documents and agreed to trade your car in, you have committed to a contract. Although it is very unlikely that the company will take action against you should you change your mind even at this late stage, it is easier to ensure your decision is correct earlier on, during the negotiation.

Before you agree to the deal, ask the sales person to confirm the figure without the part-exchange. You need to know the figure that they will "stand the car in at." This is a term dealers use for the value of the car to the business. The company may reduce this value, if it is not worth the amount they told you. Do not fear; this won't make a difference to you, because they will also reduce the price of the car you bought by the same amount.

The majority of the time it will not make any difference to the deal, whether you exchange the car or give them the money instead, but you need to confirm this before committing yourself.

An example of when it will make a difference is if the deal is based on them getting more for your car than it is worth. Imagine you have received the perfect deal:

On the road price	**£14,995**
Retailer profit	**£1,200**
Retailer registration bonus	**£500**
Discounted price	**£13,295**
Part-exchange valuation	**£3,500 (highest trade offer)**
Price to change offered	**£9,795**
Price to change agreed	**£ 9,295**

In this example, you have been offered an additional £500 to get your business. So currently they will lose £500 on the deal. They will still feel that they can get £4,000 for your car from one of their regular traders, which is why they have agreed to do it. They won't, however, if you don't trade the car in. That would mean they have given you all the profit and bonus from their car, as well as taking a £500 loss on the value of your car.

The other implication of not trading it in, when you had agreed to do so, is that already they may have promised the car to another customer or sold it to another company.

There will be no broken promises and unnecessary conversations if you have confirmed the deal is the same either way. If you tell them you may have a buyer for your car, then they won't find a buyer for it before you have decided.

I hope this helps.

Take care on the roads.

All Buyers Are Liars

About Scott Owen

 Scott Owen was born in July 1971 in the English fishing town of Grimsby, Lincolnshire. He spent his formative years abroad in the Bahamas, Greece and Dubai, where his father built a career in the oil industry.

He reluctantly returned to Grimsby when he was approaching his sixteenth birthday. Scott enrolled on a two year college course in refrigeration & air conditioning. His time at college turned out to be carefree and enjoyable. Once he had completed the course he was determined to start working rather than pursuing further education, and luckily he was offered a position with the industry's largest company – Carrier, the inventor of air conditioning.

This position took him to Biggin Hill, Kent, where he struggled to make ends meet at times, but the experience was vital in making him independent. After three years of flogging a dead financial horse, he decided his only option was to return home.

Following 12 months of unemployment, he finally got a break selling cars for a local Peugeot dealer. Working with a mentor he was highly motivated and soon learned how to build successful relationships with customers, whilst providing a professional service.

These attributes set him apart from his peers and he soon became the first person to sell 200 cars in his first year with the company.

The grass suddenly became greener for Scott with a newly built Renault dealership and he jumped ship, after a sudden rush of blood to the head. This decision was soon proved to be a poor one and after 5 months he was rescued by a friend, who ran a local refrigeration consultancy.

Scott joined Honeywell LCL in 1995 and spent the next five years working with ASDA stores on a number of new build and refurbishment projects. During this time, in 1996, Scott's father passed away after a long illness and in 1999, Scott became a father to his first son.

After he was made redundant in 2000 he found himself at the mercy of the motor industry once more. This time it would take over the next eight years of his life - providing him with laughter, tears, delight, frustration, excitement, stress and huge satisfaction as well as enormous pressure. He always proved his worth to his employers (whilst standing his ground when necessary) and sold some of the biggest marques in the industry.

After an initial spell with Mazda & Mitsubishi, he moved onto Mercedes-Benz, during which time he became a father again to his second son, born in 2004. After a clash of personalities which brought him close to a breakdown, he moved to Volkswagen, then BMW and eventually back to Mercedes-Benz. The current state of the motor trade encouraged Scott to cut his losses and look for an alternative career.

Unfortunately his timing could not have been worse, or could it?

After sending hundreds of applications with little or no response he decided to accelerate his learning of business planning to create his own company. After several months of intense research and training courses, he learned the skills to develop a strategy that would secure his financial future.

At the same time Scott decided to fulfil his lifelong ambition to write a book. Using his knowledge and experience of the motor trade, he wrote "All Buyers Are Liars" to demonstrate the sales process used within the motor trade and advise other sales people and car buyers of a very successful sales structure.

To get in touch with Scott and find out more about how he can help you and your sales team visit:

www.allbuyersareliars.co.uk

Recommended Reading

The Heart of Success – Rob Parsons – 034078623X

Persuasion - James Borg – 0273712993

Emotional Intelligence – Daniel Goleman – 0747543844

Awaken the Giant Within – Anthony Robbins – 0743409388

Give Me Time – The Mind Gym – 0316731692

The Wealthy Author: The Fast Profit Method For Writing, Publishing & Selling Your Non-Fiction Book – Joe Gregory & Debbie Jenkins - 1905430698

Persuasion Skills Black Book: Practical NLP Language Patterns for Getting the Response You Want – Rintu Basu – 190543054X

Bare Knuckle Selling: Knockout Sales Tactics They Won't Teach You At Business School – Simon Hazeldine - 1905430051

Bare Knuckle Negotiating: Knockout Negotiation Tactics They Won't Teach You At Business School – Simon Hazeldine – 1905430140

Cage Fighter: The True Story of Ian "The Machine" Freeman – Ian Freeman & Stuart Wheatman

Influence: The Psychology of Persuasion – Robert Cialdini – 006124189X

Zig Ziglar's Secrets of Closing the Sale – Zig Ziglar - 0425081028

What Every Body Is Saying: An Ex-FBI Agent's Guide to Speed-reading People – Joe Navarro – 0061438294

Get Anyone to Do Anything – David J. Lieberman – 0312270178

How to Win Friends and Influence People – Dale Carnegie – 0091906814

Dealing with People You Can't Stand: How to Bring Out the Best in People at Their Worst – Dr Rick Brinkman & Dr Rick Kirschner - 0071379441

Just Ask the Right Questions to Get What You Want – Ian Cooper – 0273712780

Getting It Done: How to Lead When You're Not in Charge – Roger Fisher & Alan Sharp – 0887309585

How to Talk to Anyone: 92 Little Tricks For Big Success In Relationships – Leil Lowndes – 0722538073

Persuasion
Skills
BLACK BOOK

Practical NLP Language Patterns for
Getting The Response You Want

Rintu Basu

FREE INSIDE
'Black Book'
Persuasion
Training
E-course

www.bookshaker.com

BARE KNUCKLE
NEGOTIATING

KNOCKOUT NEGOTIATION TACTICS THEY WON'T TEACH YOU AT BUSINESS SCHOOL

Download
FREE
'Bare Knuckle'
Bonuses

SIMON HAZELDINE
FOREWORD BY DUNCAN BANNATYNE OBE
from BBC TV's "Dragons' Den"

www.bookshaker.com

www.bookshaker.com

"The world is a dangerous place; not because of the people who are evil, but because of the people who don't do anything about it."

ALBERT EINSTEIN

A FEELING OF WORTH

A Manifesto For Mending Our Broken World

BAY JORDAN

www.bookshaker.com

14710440R00110

Printed in Poland
by Amazon Fulfillment
Poland Sp. z o.o., Wrocław